WHAT ARE THE FACTORS THAT HEAL?

What Are the Factors That Heal?

WOLFGANG GIEGERICH

DUSK OWL BOOKS
London, Ontario, Canada

ISBN-13: 978-1-9992266-2-6

Table of Contents

Sources and Abbreviations

For frequently cited sources, the following abbreviations have been used:

CW: Jung, C. G., *Collected Works.* 20 vols. Ed. Herbert Read, Michael Fordham, Gerhard Adler, and William McGuire. Trans. R. F. C. Hull. Princeton (Princeton University Press) 1957–1979. Cited by volume and, unless otherwise noted, by paragraph number.

GW: Jung, C. G., *Gesammelte Werke*, 20 vols., various editors, Olten and Freiburg im Breisgau (Walter-Verlag) 1971–1983. Cited by volume and, unless otherwise noted, by paragraph number.

Letters: Jung, C. G., *Letters.* 2 vols. Ed. Gerhard Adler. Bollingen Series XCV: 2. Princeton (Princeton University Press) 1975.

MDR: Jung, C. G., *Memories, Dreams, Reflections.* Rev. ed., Ed. Aniela Jaffé. Trans. Richard and Clara Winston. New York (Vintage Books) 1989. Cited by page number.

Erinn.: *Erinnerungen, Träume, Gedanken von C.G. Jung*, ed. by Aniela Jaffé, Zürich and Stuttgart (Rascher) 1967.

CEP: Giegerich, W., *Collected English Papers*, 6 vols. New Orleans, LA (Spring Journal Books) 2005–2013, now London and New York (Routledge), 2020.

Transl. modif.: Appearing at the end of a citation, this indicates that I modified the particular quotation from the *Collected Works* in order to bring the English translation a bit closer to the wording and spirit of Jung's original German text.

Preface

In all my publications so far I have devoted myself to theoretical reflections of psychological themes, be it the questions around the topic of the inner logic of psychology itself and the search for a rigorous notion of psychology in the Jungian tradition and with a commitment to psychology's root metaphor "soul", or be it the psychological study of particular soul phenomena from mythemes and fairy tales to aspects of modern technology. Although occasionally there may have been a few comments on practical psychotherapeutic issues in my essays or books, the practice of psychotherapy has never been a central topic. I also never published any case reports. This "avoidance" is not due to a lack of interest in actual therapeutic work with patients (which, after all, has been my profession and daily work for four decades). It is due to the fact that I think that the true purpose of psychological writings has to be the training of the mind, on the one hand, and that the focus on cases and the practice of psychotherapy is psychologically counterproductive, locking the psychological mind in the narrow confines of the consulting room, on the other hand. But, as C.G. Jung pointed out, it "is the smallest part of the psyche, and in particular of the unconscious, that presents itself in the medical consulting room",[1] which is why it is necessary to "burst the fetters which hitherto have tied [analytical psychology] to the consulting-room of the doctor".[2] As therapists we certainly need to enter the consulting room, but not with a consulting room mind. We need to gain our outlook and orientation from within the infinitely wider horizon of the soul's manifestation in mankind's whole cultural history.

But with the present book I break with the tradition outlined above and turn explicitly to the practice of psychotherapy. This does, however, not mean that in this book about "What are the

---

1   *Letters 2*, p. 307, 17 June 1956, to Nelson.
2   *CW* 16 § 174, transl. modif.

factors that heal?" the reader should expect to find a kind of manual for the clinical practitioner with advice about what works best when one is confronted with difficult cases and particular therapeutic situations. Still in keeping with my psychological rather than technical or clinical approach, this book, too, offers a *theoretical reflection* of a number of healing factors, that is, an attempt, no more, to achieve a deeper psychological under-standing of what "healing" in the realm of the soul's life actually means, if seen from within, what it is in those healing factors that has the curing effect and how and why they bring it about. Needless to say, this book does not claim to cover the whole range of the factors that might possibly heal. I concentrate on those major aspects of healing that seem most important to me and relevant to the majority of therapeutic situations.

* * *

Parts of this book in various shorter and earlier versions have been presented between 2000 and 2004 in German and English, respectively, at my Neresheim Seminars, at the Sanno-Institute, Tokyo, at the Jung-Institutes of Zurich and of Munich as well as at the Paracelsus Akademie Villach (Austria). The text of the last mentioned of these presentations has been published as "Was heilt?", in: *Heilkräfte. 7. Symposium der Paracelsus Akademie Villach*, Villach (KI-Esoterik Verlag) 2005, pp. 33–62.

Preamble

The question what really heals should actually not be asked. It is a forbidden question. It is similarly forbidden as was in the legend of the *Heinzelmännchen* (brownies or elves) of Cologne any attempt to catch a glimpse of these *Heinzelmännchen*, those "little people" that every night when they could not be seen, because people slept, came out and did the next days daily work for them, so that when the butcher, the baker, the tailor, the housewife woke up, all their work for the day had already been done. This went on until one day the nosy wife of the mayor who had always wanted to watch them, with a trick managed to get a glimpse of them. From then on they never came back, and this is why even in Cologne the butcher, the baker, the tailor, the housewife have to do their daily work all by themselves.

What it is that brings about the cure is a mystery and must be respected and treated as such. One should not try to get too close to it. C.G. Jung spoke of the psyche's tendency to cure itself. The soul is self-relation, self-generation, self-expression. This implies the fundamental removedness of the locus of the cure, or of the organ that cures, from what is accessible to our consciousness, our understanding, as well as our practical doings. It is inherent in the notion of the soul that it cannot be changed from outside; inasmuch as it is its own *making* itself, it's particular states are not subject to, not the result of, causes.[3] We cannot effect healing. Psychotherapy must proceed *indirectly*.

An image that might illustrate a bit what I mean by avertedness and indirectness—that indirectness that we need on account of the factual inaccessibility of, and our due respect for, the mystery and infinity of the soul—is taken from the Greek cult of the dead. When bringing drink offerings to the dead or to the gods of the underworld, one had to do so with one's face turned

---

3   What does indeed happen is that the soul creatively avails itself of external conditions and occasions for its own making and transforming itself. But this is something very different from being subject to a cause-and-effect relationship.

11

away. One neither did not sacrifice at all, nor did one do it directly.

* * *

Since they want to preserve the mystery of the cure and do not want to pinpoint manageable empirical factors that heal, Jungians are often very quick to resort to the concept of archetypes. Thus, for example, Adolf Guggenbühl-Craig in an article on "What works in psychotherapy?", after examining a few possible answers to this question that prove unhelpful, and thus finding himself in a dead end, remembers what the late Heinrich Fierz (Jungian chief physician of a Zürich Klinik) once had said: "In psychotherapy it is not a matter of causalities, not of cause and effect, but of *constellations*. ... *We* do not heal, *we* do not alleviate the suffering, but we can at best *constellate* healing and alleviation of the suffering." An excellent assessment, except maybe for the fact that in the end it is again *we* that (in the best case) do the constellating (but we do not have to be sticklers for precise non-ego formulations). Starting out from this idea by Heinrich Fierz, Guggenbühl goes on and connects the concept of constellation with the idea of the healer archetype as what is to be constellated. Thus, a little later, he makes the following statement: "I assume that the archetype of curing, of the healing or alleviation of the suffering, can be or should be constellated in the patient. ... The archetype of curing—which by the way is usually also the archetype of the illness—is what heals." [4]

As much as I welcome the basic tendency of this statement as well as some of the concrete ideas that Guggenbühl presents later on in his paper relating to this constellation of the archetype of healing, I find his recourse to an *archetype* in this connection counter-productive. Quite apart from the question whether archetypes can (or possibly even "should") be constellated by us, or whether it is not the other way around, namely, that it is inherent in the very concept of archetypes that they are autonomous and manifest of their own accord—or not at all,[5] I would say that

---

4   Adolf Guggenbühl-Craig, "Was wirkt in der Psychotherapie?", in: *Gorgo 28*, 1995, pp. 21–36, here pp. 25 and 26f. My translations.

5   "I never look for archetypes and don't try to find them; enough when they

the introduction of the archetype of healing in this context is an *empty duplication*. The sentence "we constellate the archetype of healing" contains no more information than the sentence "we constellate the healing process". If *we* can do the constellating of the healer archetype that heals the suffering, then it is, against Guggenbühl's explicit statement, we that bring about the healing. The detour via a purely hypothetical archetype is superfluous. This is a case in which it is necessary to use Occam's razor (that one should not introduce additional explanatory principles if the simpler ones are perfectly sufficient). In our explanations we have to stay on the level of actual phenomena that clearly show, or have shown, themselves.

It is true that by assigning the task of healing to the non-human or supra-human healer archetype a strong case is made for the indirectness in our thinking about healing and the mystery character of the cure itself, when it indeed happens. And one might even be willing to think that an empty duplication does not really hurt. But it does hurt. It inflates what is a *real* mystery into a *mystification* and thus paradoxically cheapens and destroys the sense of 'actually prevailing mystery'. With the healer archetype the mystery becomes hypostatized and personified. Now consciousness has the feeling of having to do with an at least logically always already known and defined, even if empirically invisible, causal agent or author behind the scenes. There would be only two legitimate possibilities for the introduction of the healer archetype in this context. The one would be an actual experience of the manifestation of the archetype, for example, of Asklepios or Chiron, *as specific divine or numinous PRESENCES*[6]—that is to say, not merely the experience of the empirical fact that healing has indeed occurred, about which fact it would only be *said* by us that it must be the doing of the or an archetype behind the scenes. The other possibility would be that the references to the "healer archetype", "Asklepios", etc., are merely used *poetically*, as a figurative and ennobling *façon de parler*, as metaphors for nothing else but

---

come all by themselves", wrote Jung (*Letters 2*, p.160, to Cappon, 15 March 1954).

6 It is doubtful whether this possibility actually exists in the modern world.

'event of an empirically real cure', the way that the Greek and the Roman gods and mythological figures have in the Western tradition of poetry been used for centuries.

* * *

By contrast with any recourse to the healer archetype, we do stay with the mystery if we say that it is "the soul" that heals. For, "the soul" is in our psychology not hypostatized, is not an entity and author, but simply the mythologizing name for the absolute negativity of the depth of actual, phenomenologically accessible psychological life as such.

All that psychotherapy can hope to do is to try to remove certain obstacles for the soul's curing itself and to prepare, on the accessible conscious side, attitudes and an "atmosphere" in the mind that might be conducive to the inaccessible soul's becoming active in the sense of its "self-regulation". It may well be that Heinrich Fierz's word "constellate" really tried to suggest no more than this.

The upshot of this whole discussion is that the insistence on the untouchable mystery of the cure and, consequently, on the indirectness and fundamental avertedness of the therapeutic approach, on the one hand, and the insistence on our sticking directly to actual phenomena, on the other hand, have to go together. They seem to exclude each other. But they do not, as we will see.

I. Introductory comments

Psychotherapy should not *focus* on healing or alleviating the suffering of patients. The mystery of what it is that actually heals needs to be preserved and respected. We have to view actual healing as no more than a *side effect* of our therapeutic efforts.

Nevertheless, it would make no sense for us to abstractly content ourselves with this negative answer to the question of what heals. There is a plentitude of concrete aspects concerning the everyday practice of psychotherapy that can be discussed on a pragmatic level without violating the general attitude described in my initial comments. Very generally, several distinctions have to be made concerning the healing factors. The first distinction is between two questions:

1. How and through what does healing come about? This question asks about the process and therapeutic attitudes.

2. Is there something healthy in the psyche that brings about the healing and if so, what is it? This is a question about substance, contents.

Jung once took up explicitly the question of what heals, attempting to describe, as he worded it, "the endeavours of our psychology," its "aims and results", and he "venture(d) to regard the sum total of our findings under the aspect of four stages, namely, confession, elucidation, education, and transformation" (*CW* 16 § 122). I will here not go into what precisely he meant with "these somewhat unusual terms," as he himself worded it (*ibid.*), nor will I follow his presentation and conception. But before I come to my own ideas about what heals I want to at least assemble and list a number of other ideas by various psychologists about what they considered as therapeutically necessary for healing.

- From Freud we have the concept of the three steps of 'remembering, repeating, working through'. Also the concept of the analysis of the resistances and of the transference.
- For Alfred Adler, it was not so much a technique but an

evoked content, the *Gemeinschaftsgefühl*, the communal sense, that healed.

- There is the idea that neurosis is healed through the "collision with reality," as Jung once termed it, which is also to be found in Kafka, when he had, e.g., one figure in the story, "The Judgment", say to another, "So now you know what else there was in the world besides yourself, till now you've known only about yourself!"
- Then there are the ideas by Jung that it is the Self that heals and the related idea of the soul as a self-regulating system. What could also be mentioned here is his idea of the "transcendent function."
- But above all, Jung believed that it is the symbols, the archetypal images, that bring about healing. "The main interest of my work is not concerned with the treatment of neurosis but rather with the approach to the numinous. But the fact is that the approach to the numinous is the real therapy and inasmuch as you attain to the numinous experience you are released from the curse of pathology" (*Letters 1*, p. 377, to Martin, 20 August 1945).
- Heino Gehrts, a scholar of ancient rituals, myths, fairy tales, in personal communication used to insist that we therapists ought to heal magically (through *Zaubern*), that is to say, more or less in the spirit of shamanism. Into this category belong a few cases that Jung reported, the case of a young Jewish woman whom he healed within one week (*MDR* pp. 138–140), for example. Also synchronicity as a healing factor has to be mentioned here. There is a rumor that some Jungian therapists like to put a mandala on the chair of a patient threatened by psychosis for him to sit on, which would also be a magical procedure. Another popular magical practice to be found in many Jungians is the use of the oracular technique of the Chinese *I Ching*.
- Finally I want to mention the idea by Hillman of the purpose of therapy as soul-making as well as his idea of *epistrophê*, of finding the god in the disease.

There are of course many more concepts that could be listed. But the ones mentioned suffice to give an impression of how diverse and manifold the conceptions of therapy can be and from which different perspectives one can approach it. I will not further explain nor comment on any of these ideas. Rather I want, in my own way and on the basis of my experience, to venture upon the project of drawing together a number of diverse, indeed quite varied possibilities of how therapy works. Jung in his presentation worked with the idea of stages, in other words, phases in a developmental whole where the highest stage presupposes that the earlier ones have already been passed through (be it in analysis or prior to it). What I intend to describe, by contrast, is separate possibilities of therapeutic method and effect, some of which might be compatible with each other or even complement each other, whereas others exclude each other.

A second distinction concerns the three main factors that are responsible for the differences between these methods and healing effects.

(1) The particular psychological situation of the patient, his or her personality and the character of his or her illness or psychological problem.

(2) The temperament, typology, habitual attitude—in short the personality—of the therapist.

(3) The therapist's training in and affiliation with some school of psychotherapy and the resulting basic theoretical orientation as well as, more practically, the corresponding furnishings of his or her consulting room.

It is clear that not all patients will benefit from the same type of treatment. It is also clear that not all theoretically possible ways to react to a clinical situation are available to a particular therapist. This is so simply because of his particular individuality. Each therapist is limited. And he may also on the basis of his conscious or unconscious theoretical assumptions be restricted to certain therapeutic reactions, while others might not even occur to him. The training that we all undergo is not only but also a kind of brainwashing that provides a certain mental horizon within which psychological phenomena will from then on be apperceived. It naturally makes a big difference if one starts out with a notion of psyche as "the behavior of the organism", based on the "bedrock of biology", or has, e.g., an idea of "soul" with a mythic or metaphysical depth. And naturally, if one's consulting room does not have, e.g., a couch or a sandtray, a classical Freudian setting or a sandplay therapy, respectively, will obviously not be possible.

Now coming to my views about what heals, I first of all have to distinguish three fundamentally different healing modalities and corresponding therapeutic situations:

1. Healing through **"letting go"** and **"releasing oneself"** (Chapter IV). Here the focus is on the *person* of the patient (or also of the therapist).
2. Healing through **"work on consciousness"**, work on the patient (Chapter V). This work is concerned with *object* (the illness): the complexes, the "content of neurosis" (Jung), the internal logic or structure and mechanisms of the disorder.
3. Healing through **"newness"** and **"movement as such"** (Chapter VI). In this chapter, the interest is directed to the *form* of the psychological theory or therapeutic method.

Whereas these refer to attitudinal changes, methodical work, or the condition of a method, there is also another healing factor that is a stable and permanent part of the "inventory" of therapy, if I may say so: **the personality of the therapist**. Because it is the most important factor it will be discussed before the ones just mentioned. (Chapter III).

At the end we will also have to consider **the limits set to psychotherapy**, to the attempt to heal psychological disorders (Chapter VII).

In addition I have to make two more distinctions that can apply to any of the first three therapeutic modalities just mentioned:

There are two different levels on which the healing process can go on.

a) The semantic or content level.
b) The syntactic or relation level.

And therapy can be aimed at two fundamentally different objectives:

a) A therapy in which the overall goal is for the patient to achieve **mature adulthood**, a fully developed "I" or subjectivity ("I," not "ego").

b) A therapy in which the overall goal is either **soul-making** in Hillman's sense or the **individuation process** in the specific Jungian sense (which is not the same thing as soul-making, and yet is just as different from developing the "I" as is soul-making).

Jung himself considered *his* terms "confession, elucidation, education, and transformation" "somewhat unusual". In a similar way, I am aware of the fact that my distinctions are by no means self-explanatory. What is meant will have to become clear in the course of their detailed description. Suffice it to say at the beginning that healing through "releasing oneself" and healing through "working on the patient" are almost diametrically opposed realities of therapy. But each is essential. One just has to know when and where which one is in place and when and where not. Almost the same is true about the two different objectives, the development of one's subjectivity, on the one hand, versus soul-making or individuation, on the other.

Before we can turn to the different "factors that heal" themselves, we need now, in Chapter II, to think about and clarify what the appropriate *psychological* approach to the topic of healing is that does not concretistically make our therapeutic interventions and operations in the consulting room directly responsible for healing effects, but respects the mystery of healing.

II. Two ways of thinking about healing: in medicine – in psychotherapy

I have to approach what I want to discuss in this chapter in a roundabout way. I begin with examples that have nothing directly to do with healing or with medicine and psychology in order to lay the ground for the conceptual distinctions that I want to introduce.

Nearly thirty years ago I once presented in a lecture at a theological academy my ideas about the role and function of the archaic institution of sacrificial slaughter for the emergence of human culture, the transition from animal to human existence, and the origin of what we call soul. In passing I set off my theory of sacrifices from those of Walter Burkert[7] and René Girard[8], criticizing in their views what I claimed was a naturalistic, positivistic fallacy: the attempt to explain the becoming fully human of *homo sapiens* as well as human culture from empirical causes (factors or behaviors, such as violence in behavior) that were clearly not strictly human, but rooted in biology. In the discussion of my presentation one person said he thought that what I did was much the same attempt to derive human culture from what was not human, only in different ways, by having recourse to other factors.

It is true that I too tried to explain the transition from "not human" to "human". But what the discussant overlooked was that there is a fundamental difference between two types of defining such a "transition".

The one type, which I detected in Burkert as well as Girard, believes that something totally new in the sense of representing a different, previously not existing category (here: culture and the truly human) can be derived from what does decidedly not belong to this category. What the theory of "The birth of the human mind and of human culture from biology", to put it this way, ultimately

---

7   Walter Burkert, *Homo necans. Interpretationen altgriechischer Opferriten und Mythen*, Berlin, New York (de Gruyter) 1972.
8   René Girard, *La violence et le sacré*, Paris (Bernard Grasset) 1972.

achieves is that it *reduces* the higher category of true human-ness—the mental world as such, the whole sphere of culture—to the lower category, biology, i.e., that this theory stays all the time on the lower level and eliminates the category difference altogether, while of course believing to have actually arrived at and explained the generation of the higher level.

What I had presented, by contrast, belonged to the other type of derivation. From the outset it starts out and presupposes the presence of what ultimately has to be achieved. And yet it is an account of the first time *generation* of the soul, of human culture, and humanness in general, an explanatory movement from "not available" to "available". This obvious contradiction is resolved when we do not conceive the starting point, the "not" or absence, as zero and total non-existence, but instead as "predisposition", as a "determinate not". That is to say, the intellectual process of deriving or explaining the coming into being of something categorially new begins logically from the start already on the higher level of the new category and only recounts a process taking place on this level and within this category. The lower category, in the present case the naturalistic and positivistic level of biology, has already been left behind. What this type of explanation describes is the development from "implicit" to "explicit", from *"ansichseiend"* to *"fürsichseiend"*, or a self-unfolding like that of an acorn into an oak.

Accordingly I had, to conclude this example, in my lecture about blood sacrifices spoken of the *"soul's* killing itself into being". The beginning of the argument was made with the very soul whose first generation was to be described. The soul made, pro-duced, *itself.* The soul itself was logically the subject or agent that empirically produced the soul. It was the already *human* animal—the animal that had already in principle transcended the animal level of exclusively biological existence—that in a temporal process for the first time brought about and attained its actual humanness. It is the self-actualization of something that is only *in potentia* there, a self-actualization that takes place in observable empirical steps and through observable events.

The former type of theory, on the one hand, leaps boldly across the categorial hiatus to the higher category and, on the other hand, through this very leap, denies the existence of a hiatus, thereby implicitly reducing the higher to the lower category.

Semantically it claims the higher for itself, while *logically* eliminating it. The second type of theory has, of course, a different problem. It is, as it were, tautological, or better tautegorical. Its explanation truly takes place on the higher-category level, but it cannot show at all how the higher category as such came into being in the first place. It has to presuppose it. But it is capable of performing a modest task: the phenomenological description of the logical movement taking place in the observable events that generate the explicit soul.

Another illustration of the same difference in the attempted explanation of the generation of something categorially higher is language. I will (only briefly) outline it in order for us to have two concrete examples in the back of our mind when we turn to our topic of how to conceive "healing".

The one group of theories of the genesis of language believes that language is simply the expansion of the use of signals with which certain animals communicate warnings of dangers, inform (like bees) about the location and distance of food sources, attempt to attract a mate, etc. They even consider such communications as (admittedly primitive) *language*. But it has nothing to do with language. It is, as I said, merely the use of signals, not of *words*, shared *meanings*, and, above all not of *sentences*. Signals (sounds, gestures, etc.) merely release certain behavioral responses. Both the signals and the possible responses are biologically steered, instinctual, automatic.[9] Words, by contrast, take one into the sphere of the mind, they convey ideas, concepts, and do not *in themselves* have the function of triggering a particular response (although they can be used for that, too). In themselves, they are merely to be mentally understood, comprehended. Language is fundamentally notional, *theoria*. Other, more complex theories of this type about the origin of language include specifically human gifts not to be found among animals, such as *empathizing* into others (fellow human beings), so-called "collective intentionality" (the capacity to share attention and

---

9 Apes can learn to connect individual so-called symbols (i.e., symbols in the sense of mere signs) with (again so-called) *meanings*, but they cannot form sentences. *Real* "shared meanings" (e.g., "love", "God", "time", "law", "the world", "crime") are in themselves complex, have in themselves thought character and as such implicitly (*an sich*) sentence character, not thing or event character.

intention), and try to explain the genesis of human language on this basis (e.g., Michael Tomasello[10]). Although the beginning is here made with something already specifically human, we have, however, the same problem. The origin of this "empathy" and "collective intentionality" is itself explained biologistically, in terms of evolution, that is, as natural, usage-based results, namely, as the result of the heightened dependence of early humans on joint effort to gain food. With this theory of social usage as the origin of human language one can get as far as arriving at "sharing", but one cannot explain how language can share *meanings, ideas, conceptions*. This more complex version of the first type of the theory of language remains also enclosed within the decidedly lower, positivistic sphere of the biological.

The other type of explaining the genesis of language starts out from the notion that language is a uniquely human capacity, a capacity that can even be empirically demonstrated to have its basis in the structure of the human brain and that is the medium of cultural evolution (e.g., Angela Friderici[11]). One main point is that language requires the capacity to form hierarchical patterns, which allows humans to *distinguish* elements of primary from those of secondary importance and to *connect* parts of the sentence that are separated from one another by other parts of the sentence. Actual sentences are the translation of these hierarchical structures into a linear medium, namely, the simple one-after-the-other sequence of sounds and words. Man is born with this brain structure that can achieve both tasks, which means that human beings possess it a priori.

One can empirically observe and describe how babies, who are *infants* (from Latin "not speaking"), in practical reality slowly acquire the use of language, in other words, how the transition from not speaking to speaking happens. But such observation comes always *ex post facto*. One must always wait until the infant *has* formed his first linguistic sounds, until the first little sentences have been built. And language as general human potential always already precedes the actual realization of the

---

10   Michael Tomasello, *Becoming Human: A Theory of Ontogeny*. Cambridge, MA (Harvard University Press) 2019.

11   Angela Friderici, *Language in our brain. The origins of a uniquely human capacity*, Cambridge, Massachusetts and London, England (The MIT Press) 2017.

capacity to speak. It is a factually existing "presupposition". Already babies, who definitely cannot speak, *an sich* (implicitly) *can speak.*

With these two examples of opposite ways to view the transition from "absence" to "realized presence" as background models in mind, we can now turn to the topic of this chapter, the two ways of thinking about healing. Healing is the transition from (partial) absence of health to health.

I begin with modern medicine, which follows the naturalistic, positivistic approach in trying to bring about the move from the lower, more likely[12] category (sickness, disorder, malfunction) to the higher ideal category (health) through empirical, natural means. Nowadays the standard of medical treatment is "evidence-based medicine" and observance of "disease management guidelines". The logic of medical treatment is: when such and such a disorder occurs you have to apply this one (or, depending on particular circumstances, one of these several) prescribed state-of-the-art measures. It is a *recipe* or *program* kind of thinking. To cook such and such a dish you have to do this; to produce health from out of illness you have to do this. Medicine is fundamentally utilitarian and technological in outlook. What is important in our context is that the medical mind *starts out* from the disease, from the absence, from the lower category, and strives to produce health. This is a bottom-up approach. The mind is here upward-looking, hoping, aspiring, and, to some extent, promising, partly even predicting. Health is to be produced from lack of health through *technical* means that are completely in the hands of man.

One might say here: but what else could be done? Is this not the only reasonable and more than that: necessary, indispensable approach? There is no alternative.

But psychology, if it understands itself as a psychology *with* soul, does, however, go quite differently about the question, "what heals?" For one thing, when I try to give some answers to this question in the following, I look from behind, from the situation after the fact of healing and stay behind. *When* healing has in fact happened, then I merely try to *understand* and describe what

---

12 Lack of organic order and organization is—theoretically—more likely and more basic than the complex perfect functioning of an organism.

was involved in or contributed to the cure. I do not try to turn the relation around and get mentally the psychological disorder in front of me so as to become able to *develop a strategy for attacking* it and to force a cure.[13] The utilitarian, technological interest of acquiring the means for the project of successful healing has in psychology been completely left behind. What we should *do* in order to heal, to bring about health, is of no concern. The psychotherapist is not a healer[14], as we already heard Heinrich Fierz so aptly pronounce; he is not *really* a member of the healing profession. What heals is "the soul" itself. Jung spoke of the soul as a *self*-regulating system.

So even if *empirically* the healthy soul is absent, as psychologist I start out from the higher level, from the presupposition of the healthy, self-regulating soul that has everything it needs within itself and take this as my actual standpoint. Health can only come from health, not *ex nihilo*, from absence of health. It cannot come merely from the application of the right therapeutic means, not from pragmatic usage of the appropriate human, social interactions on the empirical level, within the social arena. Psychological thinking is tautological, circular. It and its tautological approach stay on and operate within the upper level.

Since as psychotherapist I never witness or detect how,

---

13 The natural sciences, to which also medicine belongs, are endeavors to acquire *means of prediction* (i.e., what is commonly called "the laws of nature"). Scientific explanations, even those attempted in psychoanalysis, are really (retroactive) *prophecies*. "Because of this event in the past, the present situation *had to* come about." Science is under the spell of the future. Psychological understanding, by contrast, has and holds its place in the present. It looks at phenomena with a view to find out what is in them and how to interiorize them into themselves, that is, into their truth.

14 Even worse is the idea occasionally voiced among Jungians that on account of their struggling with their own wounds and complexes they are "wounded healers" and that sharing with patients their own suffering and difficulties would be helpful for the patients. Being wounded (and a therapist) does not make one a "wounded healer". To think so would be one's confusing oneself with an archetype. And therapeutically it would be a violation of the crucial demand of the analyst's abstinence. No fraternization between patient and analyst! The psychotherapist should not meet the patient on the level of his human-all-too-humanness and ordinary ego (to which his own suffering belongs), but on the level of soul. He has to remain a professional, not, of course, the way a medical doctor in his white coat is a professional, but as a soul doctor. That this can include a very intimate, deep connection is something completely different from any *sharing* with the patient, on the level of human emotions, of the therapist's private struggles with his complexes.

26

through what empirical means and methods or techniques, health is in fact *produced*, I also do not study the factors that contribute to healing *for the practical purpose* of discovering the best ways of how to manage psychological disorders and achieving therapeutic success. No wish for disease-management guidelines. The interest motivating the investigation is purely theoretical, intellectual, namely psychological, a wish to understand and respond soulfully. All the factors that contributed to a real healing cannot be repeated in a new case nor can they be applied at will; they are not at our disposal. A cure happens—or it does not happen. All the psychotherapist has to do is to *ad hoc*, in each Now, *attend to* the specific psychological *phenomena* that have shown themselves, in the Greek sense of *therapeía*, to attend to them both with his trained psychological understanding and his personal response, *without any ulterior and over-all purpose of healing the patient and alleviating his suffering from his psychic disorder.*

The Greek word from which we have our word "therapy" referred to the simple attending of the servant to the dinner guest, of the nurse to the sick person, of the priest to the god. If we follow this image, the work of the therapist is a much more modest activity than that of the doctor, the healer. He is a servant.[15] But whose servant? Not the servant of the patient, of the human being. The therapist is the servant or advocate of the objective soul.

We often call ourselves analysts. But what we really are is much more like what in chemistry is called a *catalyst* (a substance that when added facilitates a chemical reaction without itself being consumed in the catalyzed reaction), much like the attendant serving a meal does not himself participate in the meal. On the one hand, a therapist is like an ordinary craftsman. But on the other hand, taking place on the higher level of the soul or mind and having left the pragmatic utilitarian interests behind, psychotherapy and psychology in the strict sense are, of course, much more lofty. To make soul, you have to start out from soul. *De nihilo nihil fit.* You cannot reach the level of soul if you start out as ego, as civilian man, and from the horizon of the social arena, the daily life, and the human-all-too-

---

15 A servant, not a modern service provider!

27

human. Practical modesty and logical high claim are the two sides of one reality.

The modest activity of the psychotherapist is his attending to what *is*; his devoting himself to the *objective matter* at hand: *this* dream or fantasy now, *this* memory, *this* momentary situation, etc., as they come up; and it is the attending to them *each for their own sake*, that is, not as one little piece in a large puzzle. Therapy has to be *zweckfrei*, without any practical purpose, without program, *sine ira et studio*. The only purpose of psychology (psychotherapy) is to do justice, intellectually and feeling-wise, to the products and expressions of "the soul" in their eachness and individuality, that is, with each one respected as having its own dignity and fulfillment within itself. The following statement taken from Jung's late work, *Mysterium Coniunctionis*, might qualify as the maxim of the therapeutic attitude, "Above all, don't let anything from outside, that does not belong, get into it, for the fantasy-image has 'everything it needs' within itself."[16] The therapist should, as carefully as he can, attend to the *phenomenon* at hand (to 'what objectively shows itself of its own accord') and so to speak forget about everything else, about last week's session, the larger picture, the patient's biography, etc., and above all about all ego wishes and emotions. Immersion in the now, but this with one's whole heart.

It is for all these reasons that I find today's powerful interest in studying and proving the efficiency of the diverse methods of psychotherapy ruinous. This is the positivistic attempt to grip and pin down something that has a chance only when it is left untouched. Psychotherapy must take place in the (logical) negativity of "the soul". It must respect the dignity and the inner infinity of the personality, the human being. In this context, a passage from Jung comes to mind. At first, he states, "The vast majority of people are quite incapable of putting themselves individually into the soul of another", which, pointing to differences in giftedness between individuals, is not relevant for us here. But his continuation immediately thereafter more or less discounts the exceptional skill of the very few on the basis of the

---

16 C.G. Jung, *CW* 14 § 749. I have added the not unimportant words "within itself," which have been omitted in the *CW* translation, but are part of Jung's German original.

more general and fundamental notion of the on principle inaccessible otherness of others[17]:

> This is indeed a singularly rare art, and, truth to tell, it does not take us very far. Even the man whom we think we know best and who assures us himself that we understand him through and through is at bottom a stranger to us. He is *different*. The most we can do, and the best, is to have at least some inkling of his otherness, to respect it, and to guard against the outrageous stupidity of wishing to interpret it (*CW* 7 § 363, transl. modif.).

In practice, this means that we should not directly focus on the patient's agonizing symptoms, not be guided by the wish to help and heal directly, indeed to refrain completely from such a wish. The healing process *must be left to its own devices*. At the same time it means one's turning away from one's spellbound attention to what *the patient wants* first and foremost, what *he* is subjectively focused on, in order to patiently and carefully devote himself to the individual, specific psychological phenomena and situations, the dream images, the forms of pathology, which may raise completely different issues and pursue the concerns of the *objective soul*. We must learn to say goodbye inwardly to the desire to help and heal, because only in this way can we truly be psychotherapists. Jung reports that sometimes when a patient had told him all about his complaints and wanted to know what to do he answered that he, Jung, also did not know what to do. "Some of my patients 'perhaps thought I knew the magic formula, but I soon had to tell them that I did not know the answer either'" (*CW* 11 § 514). Another time we hear:

> In the majority of my cases the resources of the conscious mind are exhausted (or, in ordinary English, they are "stuck"). It is chiefly this fact that forces me to look for hidden possibilities. For I do not know what to say to the patient when he asks me, "What do you advise? What shall I do?" I don't know either. ..." (*CW* 16 § 84)

A few paragraphs later he explains what his reaction to his own not knowing was: "In such cases, then, my attention is directed more particularly to dreams" (*ibid.* § 86).

This is the turning away, with systematic awareness, from the technical stance. And in this move we see that shift that constitutes the *indirectness* of the therapeutic attitude: the attention

---

17 What a contrast to the role that empathy plays in Tomasello's biological theory of humanization!

is withdrawn from the symptom or pressing problem, that is, from what is the central concern of the patient and the only reason why he has come to the therapist in the first place, and is directed to something that has no direct relation to the patient's problems and must in many cases feel rather irrelevant to the patient.

> I have often been asked, "And what do you *do* about it?" I do nothing; there is nothing I can do except wait, with a certain trust in God, until, out of the conflict born with patience and fortitude, there emerges that particular, for me unforeseeable solution that is destined for that particular person. Not that I am passive or inactive meanwhile: I help the patient to understand all the things that the unconscious produces during the conflict (*CW* 12 § 37, transl. modif.).[18]

Psychologically, the problem with the technical approach is both the focus on *effects* (one's bringing about the cure by oneself) and the *will as such* that is its driving force behind this focus, the *will* to bring about the cure. Together they reveal one's having logically settled in the ego and that one is committed to the bottom-up approach.

---

18   Another Jung passage that comes to mind in this context is to be found in *CW* 11 §§ 35 and 36.

III. The main healing factor: the personality of the therapist

In this first chapter devoted to the identification of one of the healing factors it will have to be shown on its own if our double principle of indirectness/mystery/absolute negativity, on the one hand, and strict phenomenology, on the other hand, holds true.

I start out from a few quotations by Jung. "In psychotherapy we have gained the insight that in the last analysis it is not knowledge and the technique applied, but the personality that has a curative effect" (*CW* 17 § 240, transl. altered to reflect the original). "It is even largely immaterial what sort of technique he [the doctor, psychotherapist] uses, for what makes the difference is not the 'technique' but first of all the person who uses the method" (*CW* 10 § 337, transl. modif.). "Only what a person really is has healing power" (*CW* 7 § 258, transl. modif., Jung italicized the entire sentence). The "is" in this sentence needs to be highlighted. Furthermore: The analyst's "personality is one of the main factors in the cure" (*CW* 4 § 586). Like parents and teachers, therapists have the greatest effect through *who* they *are*, not so much through what they say.

What is essential concerning the personality of the therapist is three things: his authenticity, his inner *steadfastness*[19], and the personality's psychological depth, range, and differentiation. The first two qualities are ordinary virtues of the therapist in so far as he is conscious person and civilian man. The third of the requirements mentioned goes deeper and involves already a particular giftedness for the specific profession of a "soul doctor". Nevertheless, even this giftedness could still be understood on a rather ordinary level. Be this as it may, at any rate, the absence or presence of such a giftedness is reflected in the mental horizon within which the therapist apperceives psychological phenomena.

---

19 Concerning the topic of "steadfastness" I refer the reader to the section, "The psychotherapeutic stance towards presenting complaints" in my essay, "*Psychologie Larmoyante*. Glen Slater, for Example", in: *CEP* 4, pp. 503 f.

The crucial difference is whether one's frame of reference for the interpretation of psychological motifs is common sense, everyday reality, the social world, and the human-all-too-human desires and fears, or whether one's consciousness, in view of psychological material, is one that is informed and inspired by the objective soul. Are mythologies and the history of symbols for the psychologist only a quarry to take material from in order to pair it schematically with modern psychic phenomena—or do the "metaphysical" depth and mercurial spirit revealed in the great productions of human culture from myth and ritual to religion, philosophy, and the arts have a living and productive, indeed creative, echo in the soul of the analyst?

However, what is ultimately at stake with the emphasis on the personality of the analyst goes into an altogether different direction, into a much more *personal* and *subjective* depth than even the question of such a creative echo in the soul of the psychologist. What this means will now have to be made clear.

I start out again from very simple reflections. The *personality* of the therapist referred to is the personality precisely of the concrete human being that he or she is, the way he or she really *is*, his or her whole attitude as it actually and unintentionally shines through his or her behavior. This means that with our recourse to the personality of that human being who happens to be the patient's psychotherapist we clearly stay on the phenomenological level. And yet, what is the personality? It is not visible, not a thing, nothing that could be captured and clearly defined through empirical scientific means. Although it reveals itself (this is the phenomenological aspect), it does so only indirectly, unintentionally, as I said. We cannot catch it. As itself it never appears. It never becomes a positivity. It remains a mystery.

This is why the following statement by Jung about teachers, which applies to psychotherapists in much the same way, is a bit problematic: "It is important that the teacher should be conscious of the role he is playing. He must not be satisfied with merely pounding the curriculum into the child; he must also influence them through his personality. This latter function is at least as important as the actual teaching, if not more so in certain cases" (*CW* 17 § 107a). What Jung said here sounds (or could at least be understood) as if the teacher (or therapist) should and could have

32

explicit consciousness of, and thus access to, his own personality and deliberately use it to influence his pupils or as healing factor in his work with patients, respectively. But this is precisely not possible, and to try to get hold of one's personality in the indicated way would be futile and counterproductive. It is the very point of the personality that it exerts a real influence even if and precisely if one is not consciously aware of it and does not focus on it. Teachers have to focus on doing their regular teaching job. Therapists, likewise, have to concentrate on the psychological phenomena and do their best to work with *them*. The effect of the personality comes into the bargain, unseen, unintended, innocently.

We should read Jung's statement as simply asking for awareness of the general truth that we are more than what we do and say and intend, that in addition to all our conscious and deliberate efforts we *are*, so to speak, *"infectious"* (be it in good or in bad ways), simply through *what we are*. As human beings it is our general responsibility to take care that we are in our being, or that our personality is, not deformed by resentments, feeling-toned complexes, neurotic obsessions, etc. But in our concrete work with others we can be oblivious of personality and simply *be* it, "ride on it" like a horseman lets himself be carried by his horse.

The situation of the psychotherapist is, however, still more complex, *provided that* he wants to work on the basis of a psychology with soul. The teacher's job is more or less clearly defined. He does have the task to transmit to his pupils what the *curriculum* demands. One might think that the therapist's equivalent of the teacher's curriculum is his psychological theory, method, and techniques. He has to apply it to the case before him. But this is not so. There *is* no equivalent to the teacher's curriculum. For the psychotherapist it is essential that he does not—with what in psychoanalysis has been called the defense mechanism of *dazwischenschieben*—interpose or interject between the patient and himself a technique or method. What Jung demands of the analyst is that he does not as person, as himself, hide behind a method. He must not try "to evade from the personal confrontation with the patient's personality and to hide behind a technique" (*CW* 10 § 347, transl. modif.), not "entrench[-] (himself) behind precepts" (cf. § 335). Let us hear

another relevant passage.

> And so it happened that, long after psychotherapy had grown to a psychology, and therapeutics had ceased to be a mere technique, the illusion still continued to flourish that psychological treatment was some kind of technical procedure. It would be decidedly too optimistic to say that this illusion has ceased to exist even among the ranks of psychotherapists, nor would it accord with the facts. All that has happened is that now and then voices are heard which demur at the mechanization of psychotherapy and express their interest in removing it from the soullessness of a mere technical procedure. Their aim is to raise it to the higher plane of psychological and philosophical dialectic, where it becomes an encounter [*Auseinandersetzung*] between two psychic spheres confronting one another in their totality, that is, two human beings.[20] (*CW* 10 § 333, transl. modif.)

What Jung proposes is much more and much more radical than a merely negative move, a rejection of the application of theories and techniques because, he says, "A technique is always a soulless mechanism" (*CW* 10 § 357) and because the analyst's theoretical knowledge and technique applied are, as we already heard, "largely immaterial". Much rather, Jung demands that the psychotherapist come forward as the personality that he is; that he show his colors; that there be a direct, "naked" encounter between the two personalities of patient and analyst. I as

---

20   Jung speaks repeatedly of psychotherapy as a dialectical procedure. When in the above quote he uses the phrase "philosophical dialectic", we should not be misled and think that this is the same sense of dialectic as, for example, in Hegel, or, for that matter, in psychology as the discipline of interiority. In the beginning of his paper, "Principles of Practical Psychotherapy" (*CW* 16 § 1) he shows that he is aware of two different senses of "dialectic": "Dialectic was originally the art of conversation among the ancient philosophers, but very early became the term for the process of *creating new syntheses*." He speaks of a "reciprocal reaction [*Wechselwirkung*] with another psychic system". This superficial understanding is also the sense prevailing in the above quote where he speaks of the "encounter [*Auseinandersetzung*] between two psychic spheres confronting one another in their totality". But what *we* now mean by "dialectic" in the spirit of Hegel, Marx, and others is not the method for *creating* syntheses and does not function by bringing together or confronting *two separate* entities, items, systems. It is rather the internal and recursive self-unfolding of *one* thesis going under into its implicit self-contradiction and further into its truth. Any understanding of Jung's notion of the "transcendent function" as a dialectic in a remotely Hegelian sense suffers from the same shortcoming. See also my "'Conflict/Resolution', 'Opposites/Creative Union' versus Dialectics, and The Climb Up the Slippery Slope", in: W.G., David L. Miller, Greg Mogenson, *Dialectics & Analytical Psychology*, New Orleans (Spring Journal Books) 2005, now London and New York (Routledge) 2020, pp. 1 ff.

therapist have to give *my answer* (precisely not only to all the different explicit questions or issues of the patient, but rather) to the personality of the patient as a whole, to him as psychic sphere, and I have to give my answer as the psychic sphere or the personality that I am.[21]

This, of course, contradicts my earlier insistence on indirectness and on the mystery character of "personality". Now what is being asked for is the *direct* confrontation of, or encounter between, two souls. What appears to be a contradiction must, however, be comprehended as a dialectic (now "dialectic" in the strict modern sense). Directness and indirectness go together. The only question is how.

The therapist's personality must not come into play by making it explicit, by approaching it and trying to explore and conceptually capture it through introspection. This would be the false (external, technical) sense of directness: one's turning it into an object and content of consciousness. What psychologically is demanded is something entirely different: a stepping backwards not as a conscious act, but as a kind of *abaissement du niveau mental*. It is a recursive move, a giving up ego-control and *letting* the unknown and inaccessible psychological depth of oneself surface. In our ordinary consciousness we are mostly conventional and collective, and even if we as scientists or philosophers practice rigorous thought, we nevertheless move on the level of the universal. What Jung is concerned about, by contrast, is the ineffable individuality of the individual. The recursive move that for us is here at stake leads thus precisely in the opposite direction, namely to "our most private and most subjective life" (*CW* 10 § 315, cf. § 316). No security. No looking *into* the abyss *that one is* from the safety of a position behind railings (from the ego vantage point). It is the other way around, one's being unpredictably from behind exposed to, and becoming the mouthpiece of, the abyss. The personality is *not made conscious*. It remains invisible and unknown, unfathomable and untouched. (Here my earlier image of the Greek way of *with averted face* making offerings to the gods of the underworld and the dead may come back to mind.) It can only manifest itself indirectly in what

---

21 This must, according to footnote 14 above about this, not be confused with my sharing personal secrets or my own psychological problems and complexes with my patient.

the human person says or does.

In this sense the direct confrontation of the two psychic spheres that is demanded is the *directness of two indirectnesses*, if I may express myself this way.

Jung once bemoaned that what psychotherapy normally amounts to is: "instead of psychology, use of psychological means..." (*Letters 1*, p.535, to Thompson, 23 September 1949). A crucial idea. A psychotherapist committed to "psychology" in the sense of this statement does not *use* his personality as a psychological means, as a curative factor. If he did, psychology would not happen. Psychology in therapy happens only if instead of using anything the therapist *lets* himself *be used* by the depth of his unknown and unknowable personality and lets *it* give its "answer", its "response", to the psychic sphere of the patient in its totality, from behind or underneath himself. It is a "natural", spontaneously happening response as the simple result of a direct "clash" and contact of the two psychic spheres in their totality. It is not a deliberated response. It is more like what happens when two chemical substances touch. Not our doing, "nature's" doing. This, we have to conclude, is the happening of veritable *psychology* in psychotherapy in the sense of Jung's cited dictum. To a particular correspondent Jung once wrote: "Try to live without the ego" (*Letters 1*, p. 427, to Anonymous, 28 April 1946). This, of course, is a piece of advice given to one individual in a particular situation of this individual. But it fits our topic (even if it is also true at the same time that the I and consciousness are of great importance for therapy). Another time Jung thus wrote in a letter: "Over against our consciousness we must learn to live as it were unconsciously" (*Letters 2*, p. 386, to Vijayatunga, August 1957). We only need to replace "to live" with "to face our patients in therapy". ("To live" would assign to Jung's statement a meaning on the *existential* level. But we are here only concerned with the therapist's making *psychology* in his psychotherapeutic work, rather than applying his theoretical knowledge or techniques as "psychological means".)[22]

What Jung suggests does of course not mean that we should literally become more unconscious. We are generally unconscious

---

22 In my book *Working with Dreams. Initiation into the soul's speaking about itself* (forthcoming), Part III, chapter "The necessity of my going under", I used the metaphors of "sleepwalking" and "swimming" to describe this stance.

enough from the outset, too unconscious. What is meant is something very different: our consciously letting the responses of the "psychic sphere in its totality" that we are (which is necessarily out of reach of consciousness and can never be explicit) emerge, responses to the other "psychic sphere in its totality".

Aniela Jaffé reports[23] that once a simple young woman from far away was referred to Jung for only a single session because she suffered from almost complete insomnia. Jung found out that she suffered from an extreme perfectionism and therefore needed most of all relaxation. He talked to her, mentioned how things like sailing could be helpful, but he noticed that she did not really comprehend him. Suddenly an old song that his mother had often sung to put Jung's little sister to sleep, occurred to him, and, almost without conscious intention he began to sing or hum his words about sailing, wind, water, and relaxation to the melody of this old lullaby. Two years later he met her doctor who told him that after this one session the insomnia had completely disappeared and that he was flabbergasted how Jung could have achieved this in a single meeting.

This is a nice example of what I have been talking about. Four aspects can be distinguished.

The first is the experience of the frustration of the conscious therapeutic approach by speaking to the conscious person of the patient and the therapist's full *acceptance* of its futility, his spontaneous realization that the patient's plight was utterly out of the range of consciousness, which was the precondition for a partial *abaissement du niveau mental* on Jung's part (for Jung's becoming "selfless", empty of his personal conscious concerns) and for his ensuing openness to and trust in the deeper, consciously inaccessible soul level. The lowering of the mental niveau is, we could say, the subjective equivalent of the objective absolute-negative interiorization of phenomena into themselves.

The second aspect is the emergence of a long and completely forgotten lullaby from the depth of his soul. Here it would not be

---

23 Aniela Jaffé, *Aus Leben und Werkstatt von C.G. Jung*, Zürich and Stuttgart (Rascher) 1968, pp. 113 f. The same episode is also related in "On the frontiers of knowledge" by Georges Duplain, in: *C.G. Jung Speaking*, ed. by William McGuire and R. F. C. Hull, London (Pan Books, Picador edition) 1980, pp. 374 f.

accurate to say that *Jung* suddenly remembered it. In reality it was his being touched by the "psychic sphere in its totality" of the patient (especially by the patient's also consciously completely inaccessible plight) that brought the memory up. It was the true contact of *souls* that evoked it. We might even say that the emergence of the lullaby was not really Jung's memory at all; rather, it was the *patient's* or *her plight's* "remembering" it *in* and *through* Jung. This alone lets us understand why Jung's taking his recourse to the lullaby had a curative effect. The healing did not come about through Jung's, as it were, "injecting" the lullaby as a medicine into the patient. No, it was merely *via Jung* that *the patient's* soul *itself* remembered what had all along been in it (and in her), but from which it had become radically dissociated because of consciousness's obsession with her perfectionist worries. The cure was the conscious soul's reconnection with its own ground. Here we can learn what Jung's idea of psycho-therapy as a "dialectic process" (in his sense) and as encounter between two psychic spheres means in its deepest sense.

The third point to be made is that it was not the lullaby as such and not the words Jung used in humming the melody that made the difference. The singing of the lullaby was merely a sign for a whole atmosphere, nay, for a particular soul truth and it evoked and constellated this soul truth as an actual presence in the therapeutic session. It is the soul truth of "*falling* asleep in the certain knowledge and with the absolute confidence that this falling is held and contained by 'mother soul'[24] as all-encompassing ground of being". This is the *Urbild* of the relaxation and of "falling asleep' that the patient (whose consciousness had been irrevocably locked within itself) according to Jung's judgment needed. Its becoming a real presence in this therapy session allowed the soul's previously disrupted self-regulation to become active again and to reestablish conscious-ness's connection to its ground.

---

24 When Jung's mother sang his sister to sleep, she did not represent, for his baby sister, herself, i.e., the literal mother known to the baby from day life. In singing a lullaby to a baby a real mother, just like the therapist Jung during this particular session, merely symbolizes (vicariously represents) and *ipso facto* truly constellates the *soul ground* as 'mother', thus allowing the child to forget the conscious world with all its day world concerns and to let itself fall into the unknown depth of the soul, which is what we call "falling asleep".

The fourth aspect is the fact that Jung, the famous psychologist and university teacher, was not too proud to come forward with his innermost subjectivity and completely abandon himself to this "infantile" lullaby level. This allowed him to become the *vicarius animae*, the stand-in for the patient's own cut-off soul depth.[25] Jung as *psycho*therapist, as *soul* doctor, allowed himself to *be used* by the *patient's* own split-off deeper part as *its* representative and voice. (Mind you, Jung did not become personal, did not share his childhood memory of *his* mother and her singing *his* sister to sleep.) The interrelation between patient and therapist was only the surface appearance; only on the literal level was it one of two separate, independent persons, of question and answer. In reality it was the enactment—however with allotted roles and Jung as *catalyst*—only of the patient's own internal dissociated relation between her conscious personality and her deeper soul ground. This, the fact that it was not really an interpersonal relation, but rather, an intrapsychic one, is why what Jung, as external *vicarius*, did fit hand in glove to her psychological condition.

Instead of treating this patient *lege artis*, Jung "improvised" in a deeper than the usual sense. From here we can understand Jung's advice to his pupils, for example, concerning the work with a patient's dream: "'Learn as much as you can about symbols and forget it all when you are analysing a dream.'" (*CW* 18 § 483) Forget it all! Learn all about psychological theories, diagnoses, techniques, but forget it all when with a patient.

The real problem with any application of such learned information, just as with the application of all theories, methods, or techniques, is that behind them "the human being *vanishes*" and that these theories and methods "always remain[-] the same no matter whether X, Y, or Z practices (them)" (*CW* 10 § 350, transl. modif.). But what is needed is precisely "the most subjective, most private, most personal" of the real X, of the real Y, of the real Z, namely the presence, through them, of the unknown and inaccessible soul ground. In the same passage Jung criticizes psychoanalysis (but it probably applies in different ways to training in all schools of depth psychology, also to Jungian

---

25 I introduced the phrase *vicarius animae* in my "*Psychologie Larmoyante*. Glen Slater, For Example. On psychology's Failure to Face the Modern World", in CEP 4, pp. 501–530, here pp. 504 and 511.

training) saying that, "Apparently the purpose of his training analysis is to make him [the trainee] not a human being but a correct applier of technique". For the same reason all these efficacy studies for the various schools of psychotherapy are disastrous from a psychological point of view. They are a clear case of the systematic exclusion of the subjective factor, the subject, the personality. One is reminded of what Jung had to say about the sciences in general. They "represent the results of their investigations as though these had come into existence without *man's intervention*, in such a way that *the indispensable collaboration of the psyche* remains invisible" (*CW* 10 § 498, transl. modif., my italics). In the sciences this exclusion of the subject, the personality, is necessary and legitimate. In psychotherapy, however, it is the substitution of methods and techniques for *psychology*, the happening of psychology.

In psychotherapy empathy, feeling into the patient, and mirroring in one's own words the feelings assumed to be present in the patient play an important role. In our context we have to note that this is also an application of a technique. The therapist, by mirroring in articulated form the empathetically detected feelings of the patient, which the patient is maybe unable to give articulation to, is therapist, but he, as the human being, as the real personality that he is, has *vanished* behind his empathizing. In his articulating the patient's (surmised) feelings he talks *about* those feelings; he gives a *report* about them and his perception of them, which means that he has left them behind and they have become objects or contents of consciousness for him. There is now a double distance. He as subject and human being is out of the feeling and by mirroring the patient's feeling for the patient, he as therapist keeps the patient clearly vis-à-vis himself. Empathizing stresses the gap between therapist and patient.

From Jung's behavior in the above example, although it is not the best example for what I want to discuss here, we can learn that there is a very different possibility for the therapist: he can stay *in* the (mode of) feeling and simply *feel* (be feeling) it. Then it is not the patient's feeling, but his own. And instead of mirroring something to the patient, he has "the same" feeling; his own feeling *is* the patient's feeling, so that the patient's feeling is what really creates unity between them in this moment. This is only possible through feeling, that is to say, *feeling* the feeling, dwelling in the mode feeling, letting the feeling prevail as a real presence, *not* by empathizing the feelings the patient has. This is a fundamental difference. From my work with supervisees and colleagues and in seminars, and from what I have seen of the psychotherapeutic literature I get the impression, that while often a lot of fuss is made about feel*ings* and emotions and a lot of indulging in them is popular, feeling as *to feel* remains pretty much unknown or at least undervalued. The former belongs entirely to the ego level; the latter is the gate to the soul. And it needs the presence of the therapist as personality, of him in his utter subjectivity—or should we rather put it the other way around and say: this real *feeling* the feeling[26] is what in the first place constellates the real presence of the therapist in his (or *as*) personality, subjectivity, and personal humanness? At any rate, it needs the courage to simply *feel* without feeling ashamed of this manifestation of his human *weakness* and without *doing* anything.[27]

As we heard, Jung wanted a psychologically conceived psychotherapy to be "an encounter [*Auseinandersetzung*] between two psychic spheres confronting one another in their totality, that is, two human beings". So far I have only stressed that this means that the therapist must come forward with his most subjective personality. But there is also a very different, almost opposite aspect that needs to be considered, and again I take my cue from Jung. He wrote in *MDR* (p. 134) that the analyst must ask himself "what kind of message the patient is *bringing me*. What does he *mean to me?*" (my emphases). In other words, it is therapeutically essential that the therapist is not only moved by personal sympathy and empathy for this patient, all of which belong to the ego level, but also takes a real personal intellectual interest in the material of this patient, in the objective substance of the human problem that the patient psychologically represents for him. If the analyst's own curiosity is stimulated, this has the consequence that the therapist is fully open to and truly, wholeheartedly, relating to the "soul" substance, and not only on the human level to the person, i.e., the ego, of the patient in the

---

26 "Having feelings" and "feeling (whatever it is that is to be felt)" exclude each other.

27 As to *"doing* anything": Jung's humming the lullaby melody was not a therapeutic measure taken by him, but simply the *self*-expression of the feeling that prevailed.

sense of what is usually called empathy. The patient is "bringing" him something, there is some personal (immaterial) benefit for the therapist. We can connect this also with Freud's statement about the *Junktim zwischen Heilen und Forschen* ("In psycho-analysis there has existed from the very first an inseparable bond between cure and research. Knowledge brought therapeutic success. It was impossible to treat a patient without learning something new; it was impossible to gain fresh insight without perceiving its beneficent results."[28]) Above I spoke, in the context of the discussion of the artificiality of the therapeutic situation, of the asymmetrical nature of the relation between patient and analyst. What I have pointed to now as this different aspect of "the therapist as a therapeutic factor" is the clear counterpart to the asymmetry. With it, the analyst becomes personally inter-ested and involved in the therapeutic process.

---

28 Sigmund Freud, *The Question Of Lay Analysis*, Translated from the German and Edited by James Strachey. Garden City, New York (Anchor Books, Doubleday & Company) 1964, p. 109.

IV. The healing effect of releasing oneself

I will discuss five distinct types of releasing oneself:

1. Releasing oneself as entrusting oneself to another person, the therapist.
2. Releasing oneself into the soul's self-movement.
3. Releasing one's illness from one's subjectivity into an objective Universal.
4. Releasing oneself into *oneself*, into one's own being or nature.
5. Releasing oneself into one's pathology and the notion of oneself into the notion.

1. Releasing oneself as entrusting oneself to another person: Or: the *position* of therapist in the syntax of therapy as therapeutic factor.

The most simple form of entrusting oneself is what Jung in his discussion termed "confession", one's confiding to the other person, the therapist, the intimate secret feelings and stories that one used to carry around with oneself enclosed in one's chest. It is an act of communicating, sharing something with an other. This in itself has a relieving effect. What is communicated here is concrete *contents* which are already conscious to the individual.

A deeper, less tangible and thus more soulful form is to open *oneself* to the other person. Here it is no longer this or that *content* that is shared, but one's heart, one's soul, one's very self is opened to the other. A meeting of souls (of two psychic spheres in their totality), their touching each other. Through this contact the patient's soul is potentially freed from its imprisonment within itself, its isolation, and its pointless circling in itself as in a vicious circle. This can already contribute to a dissolution of its deadlock.

Now I want to discuss these two possibilities. The psychological significance of confiding one's secret to the other person is that only in this way does this content become *real* for oneself. Many patients think they do not need to talk in analysis about certain things because *they* know them and these contents are thus fully conscious and precisely not unconscious. But this is a superficial idea, more than that, a complete misunderstanding of what being conscious means, the confounding of 'having knowledge or being aware of' something with 'being conscious of' it in a psychological sense.

Psychologically, my own knowing these things does not count. If only I know my secret[29], it is psychologically still in the state of potentiality and non-committal; it is not real, and not really conscious, either. It is my own very subjective property and thus, psychologically, fully under my control, safely encased; I can easily push it aside, not take it so seriously, treat it more like a mere idea, a fantasy, something aesthetic, a soap bubble. The secret content becomes a reality for me only when I have communicated it out loud, i.e., when I have *released* it from the containment in my own subjectivity, from the status of my private inner property. Having said it to my analyst it has left the realm of my jurisdiction. It is now out of my hands. Only this makes it objective, a real truth.

Before, its *unseenness* (by others), if I may say so, its not yet having been seen or heard, had drawn a magical circle around it. This is the problem of keeping something secret.[30] But having

---

29 What I say here about the meaning of "being conscious of ..." applies only to contents that one keeps secret or would like to keep secret, especially because they are embarrassing.

30 "The possession of secrets acts like a psychic poison that alienates their possessor from the community" (*CW* 16 § 124). But we must add here that this is only the one meaning that secrets can have for the psyche or the one type of secrets. The other essential and completely different meaning of secret is that "It is important to have a secret ... It fills life with something impersonal, a *numinosum*" (*MDR* p. 356). This is "secret" in the sense of numinous or religious mysteries. They are the *real* secrets. "But the real secrets cannot be revealed. ... It is not we who have secrets, it is the real secrets that have us" (*CW* 10 § 886). They are what one is ritually *initiated* into or that reveal themselves to oneself through deep inner personal experience. Such secrets are essential treasures for a person and give it a firm ground as an individual. "There is no better means of intensifying the treasured feeling of individuality than the possession of a secret which the individual is pledged to guard" (*ibid.*, p. 342).

uttered it, it is out in the open. I have opened Pandora's box and can never get what escaped from it back under the lid of the box. I cannot manipulate it any longer and I have no control over what the other person thinks or does with it or what it does to him. *Now* it is real. I have a witness, a *Mitwisser* (someone who is in the know). Now that the other person knows it, my secret has been released from Pandora's box and thus has become like a virus that is no longer safely contained so that it is all around me and I am exposed to its unforeseeable impact. Now I am under *its* jurisdiction. It passes sentence upon me. It *stares* at me, *hits* me, comes home to me, works on me. Now, as a "released virus", it has been released into its truth and has become *objective fact*. Truth in the psychological sense is only what has the potential to penetrate and hurt me. And only as objective fact, as truth, has it become *really* conscious. Now I have to face it and react to it, do something about it.

This is also why the idea that one could analyze oneself is false. "There are analysts", Jung once pointed out (*CW* 4 § 449), and, we might add, there are of course also many other people, "who believe that they can get along with a self-analysis. This is Munchausen psychology, and they will certainly remain stuck. They forget that one of the most important therapeutically effective factors is *subjecting yourself to the objective judgment of another*. As regards ourselves we remain blind ..." (my italics).

Here we become aware of the crucial psychological insight that at least for emotionally delicate, problematic contents, if they are to become really (psychologically) conscious, *two* consciousnesses are needed! (Neutral contents, by contrast, can be conscious enough in a more pragmatic sense even if they are not shared with some other, because here there is no wish or need to keep them secret. Because one would not mind in the least to talk about them, it is *psychologically* as good as if one *had* talked about them. But qua neutral contents, they need not and cannot be *psychologically* conscious, simply because in contrast to psychologically touchy topics they belong to the everyday ego sphere, the realm of pragmatic matters, and as such have no relevance for the soul to begin with.)

Consciousness in the psychological sense is in itself communal. I spoke of a *Mitwisser*, which reminds us of the fact that quite literally translated it could be rendered as a "con-scious (person)", an other who "knows *with*" me or "*also* knows". This in turn reminds us of the fact that the Greek and Latin words for consciousness, *syneídêsis* and *conscientia*, both contain this "with" (*syn-*, *con-*) in addition to the idea of knowing.[31] Consciousness is not simple knowing, not mere "primitive awareness".[32]

So the confession of one's secret feelings and fantasies is already a first type of stepping out of the abstract self-identity of the subject; and one's opening oneself (one's innermost being) to the other person is the same to a higher degree. In both cases it is a step from the One to the Two. The Two is the first immediacy of what I call the psychological difference, the difference between the person and "his or her soul," between me and the objective psyche. "The soul" does no longer insist on being just itself, enclosed within itself as the *anima alba*, but begins to let itself in for a new kind of identity, the identity of itself *and* its other; this also means the identity of its identity and its difference.

This is the move from immediate consciousness to self-consciousness in Hegel's sense—and only this is psychologically real consciousness. In self-consciousness we have, as Hegel put it, an I that is We and a We that is I (which is another manifestation of the psychological difference). From Hölderlin we have the formulation: "*seit ein Gespräch wir sind und hören voneinander*"[33] (ever since we *are* a dialogue, *are* communication, since we exist *as* conversation and hear from each other). In neurosis, individuality and consciousness are objectively, factually, still conceived in a reifying style, after the model of things, as self-enclosed entities. But consciousness is *in itself* self-consciousness and as such not substance, but subjectivity, and subjectivity is essentially extended, opened up toward ..., or a *relation to* ... It is not merely my private interior, but is in itself 'public', communal.

Hölderlin's thesis may open our eyes to the fact that a

---

31 I must admit that the "with" in these ancient words did not refer to another person who is also, along with me, in the know, as it is necessary for psychological consciousness.

32 The phrase "primitive awareness" comes from Jung, who contrasted it with true psychological consciousness, but in a sense different from the one implied here. See my "The future potential of the I. From *psychic* awareness to *psychological* consciousness", Chapter Four of my *The Historical Emergence of the I. Essays about One Chapter in the History of the Soul*, London, Ontario (Dusk Owl Books) 2020.

33 Friedrich Hölderlin in his hymn "Friedensfeier" (1802/1803).

confession is ultimately our releasing our inner secrets or even ourselves into *speech, language.* This is more than mere relationship, communication, interpersonal connection between existing beings. The move to language is the move into an entirely different dimension, the move from positivity to negativity, from ontology to *logos,* from substance to subjectivity. Language is not interrelation, but *in itself* and *objectively* relatedness as such, and thus *the sine qua non of* subjective interrelation or personal relationships.

In the therapeutic setting, the therapist represents symbolically the non-I. This non-I is not the wholly other, the other in the modern sense of Buber, Rosenzweig, let alone of Lévinas, etc. It is, as non-I, an other that has still some of the sublated I in it: it is my own other, the other of myself. So what we get here is not the I/Thou relationship of Buber and others, but the I/non-I relationship. It is *not intersubjectivity,* and yet not the solipsism of a self-identical I. It is the relation of self-consciousness: the therapeutic relationship between patient and analyst as a whole is the enactment, and the visual symbolic representation, of the I that is We and the We that is I. Modern intersubjectivity, by contrast, is based on the modern intentional logic of the unbridgeable difference, in which the individual is the absolutely isolated, atomic I that needs the other, a thou, from outside, whereas self-consciousness is reflexive, based on the traditional metaphysical (reflexive) logic of the copula as the ground that a priori conjoins the I with the other (although only ultimately, metaphysically, not immediately in everyday life).

By way of a digression I add here a few additional comments. From what I said we get one glimpse of the reason why the special therapeutic relationship, in contrast to a normal social relationship, is necessary for therapy. Often patients have told their spouses or friends the same things that they now tell the analyst, and sometimes the reaction from those persons was perhaps pretty much the same as what now the analyst says. And yet, in the one case it did not work therapeutically, in the other it does. It is essential for therapy that the Two is *not* the Two of a normal, natural, social relationship. Because such a relationship tends automatically to be an I/Thou relationship. Therapy has to be *contra naturam* and thus take place in the *artificiality* of the "consulting room". The consulting room is the concrete symbolization of the *vas Hermeticum* of alchemy, the alchemical vessel, which has to be and stay 'hermetically' sealed (i.e., sealed with the sign of Hermes) so that nothing can escape from it. Therapy has to take place, as it were, under "artificial laboratory conditions". The artificiality of the relationship is indispensable. Only then can it become a psychological relationship: a self-relation of "the soul" to itself, which unfolds into itself and its own other. This self-relation of "the soul" is, as indicated, enacted in therapy as the relationship of two real people. Because the real Thou that the therapist is is not meant, is not aimed at, he can be the representative of the non-I. And the I (the patient) can in turn be affected by the negativity of the non-I and become negative itself. Both persons in the consulting room are not identical with the real persons they are outside in their positivity. The whole relationship thus takes place in negativity, that is to say, as a relationship that is in itself logically negated and that as such is a psychological or soul relationship. Even if the two persons may not explicitly understand it as such, it can nevertheless unconsciously work as such a self-relation of "the soul". This type of relationship is what *conventionally* is called transference relationship.

The necessity of the possibility for the therapist, despite his being a real person and ordinary human being, *not* to be apperceived by the patient's soul as ordinary human being ("civilian man"), but psychologically as the soul's own other is the deeper, psychological reason for the psychoanalytical rule, established by Freud, of *abstinence,* abstinence above all in the later much narrower and a bit superficial sense of abstaining from acting out any narcissistic erotic desires, be it on the part of the patient or the analyst. Any interpersonal feeling relationship, let alone sexual relationship, would amount to a regression to the level of ordinary I/Thou relationship and, alchemically speaking, to a breaking of the alchemical vessel.

In extension of what I said about the necessity of the arti-ficiality of therapy, the *asymmetrical nature* of the relation between patient and therapist needs to be noted. It is decisive for the effectiveness of therapy. It is the patient who opens up his or her innermost self. Only he or she is the topic, not both persons. And they are not friends, buddies, partners. The patient comes only to the therapist for a service from him, a service for which the patient has to pay and with which the therapist *only* carries out his profession and earns his living. Psychotherapy is not performed out of human kindness, altruism, Christian charity. The nonetheless existing intimacy of the therapeutic relationship, despite the job-nature of therapy, is again *contra naturam*, unnatural. If it were otherwise, the relationship would be reabsorbed into the logic of everyday social life and the negativity of "the soul" would be lost. A therapist heals not only and not in the first place because he or she is so clever, so well trained, has such a deep understanding of psychology and can work so well with it. Nor because of his empathy, compassion, and humanitarian interests. The first healing aspect provided by the therapist is the fact that in his or her relation to the patient he or she has the logical *status* of a professional service provider in the artificial space of the consulting room and not that of a fellow human being. The mere fact of the laboratory situation—the *contradiction* between ordinary professional practice and psychic, soulful intimacy—is in itself one therapeutic factor.

Returning from my digression to the main subject of this section, the healing effect of one's opening oneself up to an other, I now come to a second, deeper aspect of the move from the One to Two and of the therapist's role as the representative of the other for the patient within the whole of self-consciousness. In order to understand this it is necessary to realize what a psychological illness, e.g., a neurosis, involves.

A neurosis and many other psychological illnesses draw a magical circle around the consciousness of the patient in which this consciousness is hopelessly enclosed. It is a world unto itself, pretty much immunized to the outside and to others, inaccessible to reason and arguments. The word "idiot" comes from a Greek word that primarily means the private person, the layman or non-specialist. But it can also refer to someone who lives enclosed within his own private world, not in the common world. This self-enclosure is what happens in neurosis. Neurosis cocoons the person in his or her private world and tends to try to draw into its own magic circle all experiences of reality relevant to the specific topic of the neurosis.[34] This means more than just being shut off

---

34 Here it is necessary to specify that a neurosis usually claims the neurotic patient only partially for itself. Some or even many aspects of life continue unaffected by the neurosis. It is only in those particular times and with

from the outside world. It also means that it is in itself, in its own internal movement, a vicious circle without exit. It is self-referential, indeed, an infinite loop.

It has often been pointed out that when people in a desert or primal forest want to go in a certain direction, they find out after a while that they have unwittingly walked in a circle and returned to their starting point. Neurosis is this kind of a desert or primal forest that makes you circle round within itself and does not offer any directedness, linearity, teleology, that might lead out of the magic circle, which in a temporal sense also means that it can go on forever. Life is teleological. It is a development and ultimately a heading for its end. Not so neurosis. It does not have within itself a developmental pattern that would make it go through several stages and ultimately head for its end. It is endless. What Jung called the soul's self-regulation has become inoperative in neurosis. Jung's term includes the self-relation as which the healthy soul exists.

One might think here of the motif of the so-called underworld "punishments": the fifty daughters of King Danaos were in the underworld condemned to fill with water a barrel without a bottom; Sisyphus had to roll a rock up a hill that would inevitably roll down again just prior to reaching the top; or, outside the underworld, Prometheus was chained to a rock, an eagle was eating his liver, but the liver would grow back all the time so that this process could go on forever.

In this situation of the vicious circle, the therapist serves as a *real external referent* on the level of soul at which "the soul" of the patient can moor, with which it can dock. The soul all of a sudden has a fixed point outside the desert or primal forest. Now there is a direction. The self-enclosed circle has been forced open into a straight line. This is what also entails the possibility that from now on there might through the soul's reestablished self-regulation be a *development* of the neurosis that might lead to its end.

Sometimes analysis is compared to a descent into the underworld. If one wants to follow this idea, one has to add, however, that this particular descent is not for the purpose of recovering archetypal treasures, thus particular knowledge

---

respect to those topics or situations that are crucial for the neurosis that the person of the patient is cocooned within the magic circle of the neurosis.

known only to a dead person, or wisdom from the underworld, but, conversely, in order to release "the soul" from the circularity of the movement there.

It is important here not to think of the therapist as the particular empirical person that he or she is. What I discussed here has nothing to do with the concrete human being, the distinct personality, not with relationship feelings, subjective so-called transference reactions that might be constellated by the therapist. No, we have to hold ourselves here on an abstract logical level, the level of soul. It is the *syntax* of therapy, the *logical structure or form* of the therapeutic relation as such, that provides the external referent for "the soul" caught in the magic circle of neurosis. So "the therapist" here means no more than the abstract, formal *position* or *place* of therapist in the syntax of therapy, prior to who and how the person who fills this position might be. And the therapist can *be* the real referent only to the extent that he or she is apperceived by the patient not only and first of all as particular person, but as abstract position, the logical position of the referent as such, quite apart from specific individual contents. What we are concerned with here is the **logical infrastructure** prevailing in the patient and its transformation through the simple fact of the patient's going into therapy and opening up to the other as such (i.e., not through particular therapeutic interventions on the part of the analyst or diverse happenings and processes in the course therapy).

I take the opportunity to add here a general comment: *Therapy is a ritual*,[35] and the purpose of rituals is the transformation of the *logic* of our being-in-the-world through and in *empirical* enactments. This by the way is the difference between medicine and psychotherapy. Whereas true psychotherapy is work upon the underlying invisible logic—the attempt to change the logical infrastructure—modern medicine wants to change directly the positive substrate. This is what makes psychotherapy soul-work and distinguishes it from technical approaches (e.g., cognitive

---

35 This is the main point also made by Adolf Guggenbühl-Craig in his cited paper (see footnote 4). For him it is the ritual character of psychotherapy (its methods, techniques together with the corresponding theories as mythologies) that constellates the *archetype* of the healer. I do not need this recourse to an archetype and for me the ritual character is only one possible healing factor among several.

behavior therapy).

Simply through the existence and reality of the therapist as the guarantor of the soul-internal external referent, the idea of a real outside of the magic circle is provided for the neurotic soul and thus a logical pathway is opened up for it upon which it can move out of its containment within itself, out of its self-referentiality. This change of the logical infrastructure from circularity to linearity and thus teleological development is again only possible because the therapeutic relationship is not normal social, but an artificial, relationship. Now we see that one aspect of the task of this artificiality is that it has to *prevent* the therapist and the relationship itself from being totally absorbed by empirical, social reality, which is what would be the normal thing. The therapist must not be totally identified with the particular person that he or she is. At least subliminally, implicitly, the therapist must also be apperceived as a mere position, placeholder on an abstract logical level. The fact that in therapy the patient is willing to intimately open up to another person who, however, offers himself or herself for this intimacy only by way of a professional service and for money and who on his part will not open up to the patient in the same way, describes the artificiality. This artificiality is what makes it possible that in therapy the therapist is at once experienced as the particular person, the empirical human being or civilian man sitting face to face with the patient, *and* abstractly, that is, on the soul level, as the logical placeholder, THE therapist. So the psychological *difference* is inherent in the very structure or syntax of therapy, here as the difference between the empirical-social and the logical level. And because this difference is experienced in one and the same it has the form of a logical contradiction. This maintained contradiction is an in itself therapeutically productive tension.

The fact that the therapist is not only the concrete person that he or she is on the empirical level, but also the real representation of the logic of the referent explains why, e.g., in sandplay therapy the therapist is a therapeutic factor despite his perhaps not saying or doing anything, but merely being present. It is the mere, but *real* presence of the *idea* or *figure* or *place* of therapist that is an important healing factor. If the patient would construct a sandplay picture just alone or in his family, it would not have the same effect.[36] On the other hand, a patient who is in therapy can do a sandplay or a painting from the unconscious or can have dreams at night (outside the therapeutic sessions) and yet do it within the therapeutic relationship, because the therapist as a logical figure can be really present in "the soul" even when he or she is not physically or literally present. The therapeutic relationship may extend beyond the consulting room into the patient's daily life. The sandplay, painting, or dreaming activity is then still moored at the therapist and directed towards him or her. So one is not merely playing chess with oneself. There is an extendedness out.

We often overestimate the importance of ourselves as therapists, of what we do and say, whether we correctly understand the patient, this dream of his, the transference situation, etc., and of whether our interpretations and reactions were correct and whether one should use this method and technique or that. Of course, all this is not totally unimportant. But I tend to think that for the healing process it is of less importance than the logic or structure of therapy itself, therapy

---

36 Here we have to mention an example that seems to refute what I just explained. What I am referring to is the fact that C.G. Jung during the severe crisis into which he fell after his separation from Freud started to play like children in the sand or rather with pebbles and stones, building cottages, a castle, a whole village (see *MDR* pp.173 ff.). And his devoted playing had certainly a real therapeutic effect for him. However, this example does not really refute my assertion. Jung intuitively, unwittingly, went about, as he put it himself, his "playing childish games" *as the born psychologist that he was*. His producing these "sandplay pictures" happened in the clear *artificiality* of a self-therapy, in which Jung, as the born psychologist, was able to truly *be* professional therapist and patient at the same time. He was—and this is outstanding, truly exceptional, absolutely amazing—actually capable of maintaining the psychological difference as living contradiction within himself, and precisely not as a fake psychological difference in the sense of one's constantly switching from the therapist side to the patient side and back (which would keep them neatly apart and thus allow one to escape the contradiction). We see the same therapeutic artificiality and the "therapist"/"fantasizing patient" tension also quite distinctly at work in the processes described in his *Red Book*. But particularly the *Red Book* also shows the limitation of his self-therapy. Despite his being capable of within himself holding the tension of the psychological difference of professional therapist and experiencing patient, *ultimately* his solitary process is subject to his own critique of self-analysis as "Munchausen psychology" (see above p. 44): "As regards ourselves we remain blind, despite everything and everybody" (*CW* 4 § 449).

as *objective institution and ritual* with the therapist as the mere representative of a *logical position*. Oftentimes I think in a therapy that now we have really analyzed the core of the patient's problem. And then it turns out that this did not make any difference. And conversely, I often hear that a small comment that I made and that I did not attribute any importance to at the time, and that now, I in fact did not even remember having made, was so important for the patient and made all the difference. So I think we should not take ourselves and what we do in therapy too seriously. We are not really all that important. At any rate, there is no direct relationship between what we say and do and the therapeutic result.

I compared neurosis with a desert or primal forest in which one's movement will always be circular. We could also say with another image that a neurosis is up in the clouds, on the moon, in the realm of mere potentiality, in cloud-cuckoo-land. This is the realm of "the soul" in which everything is simultaneous, so that all ideas, moments, insights neutralize each other and nothing has a real consequence. This is why there is no movement and nothing happens. The opposites coexist in the soul. Contradictions do by no means cancel each other out or lead to a clash the way it would inevitably be in the real world. The pure world of the soul has room for everything, even if it be mutually exclusive, at the same time. This is the reason why in this realm there is no movement; nothing happens. Only when the soul has become immersed in reality do successiveness and the exclusion of opposites originate. As a small example for the peaceful coexistence of conflicting individual moments of a neurosis I mention a mother complex. One blames one's mother (1), but at the same time feels guilty for blaming her (2), and in addition one also excuses her and sympathizes with her (3). The opposite emotions exist simultaneously without canceling each other.

With having a therapist, all of a sudden a real vis-à-vis exists psychologically, that is, logically. And with this, the cloudy soul (the *anima alba*) and its hazy contents have received an anchor in sublunar reality. This provides the transition from the soul's circular time as simultaneity to the linear *time as succession* and to an Either/Or. Now the realm of the temporal can also *psychologically* be entered. It becomes possible to look at *one* feeling or aspect *at a time*, and to distinctly *retain* the notion of it when it becomes necessary to experience their opposition, so that through their simultaneity in the mind their mutual exclusiveness can be experienced as a *real* opposition, indeed, contradiction, that requires some kind of resolution.

In addition, the diffuse conglomerate of feelings and ideas can now be broken down into its components and into the distinct aspects of each component; the real vis-à-vis of the therapeutic situation *provides the logical infrastructure* through which the opposite sides of ambivalences can indeed be placed to different sides and thus be kept separate, maybe even distributed onto the two figures present in therapy. The patient in this way is forced and enabled to take an unambiguous stance, to take one side and think it through; in the course of time maybe opposite stances, but only one at a time, one after the other. The logical infrastructure inherent in the therapeutic setting is the embodiment of the logic of confrontation and vis-à-vis, of the capability to take issue with one's own impulses, ideas, fantasies, and to critically reflect them. In the therapist as the witness, the *Mit-wisser*, the neurotic patient has the continuously persevering consciousness that is lacking in neurosis. The therapist represents consciousness as *objective* position, as a vis-à-vis that is not at one's disposal, as the instance or agency of judgment and truth. Thus a development and, together with this, ultimately an exit out of neurosis becomes logically feasible.

At the end of this section I want to emphasize once more that the curing factor discussed here precedes, and has nothing to do with, any measures taken by the therapist in the consulting room, any doings, therapeutic procedures, interventions, methods of his, etc. It is, rather, the quiet, motionless logic of the institution of therapy as such that has a beneficial therapeutic effect.[37] This distinguishes "the therapist" as discussed here from "the therapist" as viewed in Chapter III, where the focus was precisely on the *personality* of the therapist. But the title *vicarius animae* applies to both, but of course in very different ways. The therapist became *vicarius animae* in Chapter III precisely only if and when he personally and in concrete situations became receptive for and was used by the patient's deeper soul needs for

---

37 This is what, in addition to other features, gives to therapy its character as *ritual*.

their expression. In the present section, however, it is the *abstract position* of therapist within the whole of the therapeutic setting that objectively holds the office of *vicarius animae* in an imperceptible, only implicit way, precisely regardless of whether the specific person of the therapist possesses a deeper soul sensitivity and views the psychological phenomena truly psychologically (within the horizon of the objective, cultural soul) or not.

2. Releasing *oneself* into "the soul's" self-movement or: Interiorization into "the soul"

In the first sub-chapter we were still very much at the outside edge or threshold of therapy. We were concerned with the question of the therapeutic effect of the patient's decision and willingness to go into therapy and open up to a therapist; and we were concerned with one aspect of the general structure of the institution of therapy as such, the logical place of "therapist" within this structure. Now the entrance into therapy lies behind us and we want to see what works therapeutically within the therapeutic process or how that process itself works.

The main factor here is that (or whether and to what degree) the psyche of the patient is willing to release itself into the therapeutic process. We have to distinguish between the willingness to enter therapy and to open up to the other person, on the one hand, and the readiness to release *oneself* into the actual therapeutic process, on the other. Some patients come very regularly to the therapy sessions, maybe even bring some real sacrifice in order to be able to come (such as the great financial expense or a long, time-consuming journey from where they live), and yet they do not really want to get *into* therapy. They are like people who want to learn how to swim and come to a swimming pool but do not want to get into the water, do not want to get wet.

But one most important therapeutic factor in therapy is precisely this getting wet, this jumping into the water. In alchemy we have, for this essential move, the image of diving into or rather of the submersion in the bath. It is the immersion in the objective soul, in the world of images. In swimming one allows oneself to be carried by the element of water, that very element of which one *knows* that it is *not* a solid ground on which one could stand and walk, but an element that when one puts one's feet on it gives way and in which bodies are likely to sink and people can possibly drown. In order to swim one has to give up one's wish to stand upright, heads up, so that one can face the world, and along with it one has to sacrifice one's ego control. Instead one has to lay the full length of one's body flat onto the surface of that unstable element. And then one experiences the miracle that the water will support and carry the body, the same body that used to sink into it when one stepped into the water.

Underlying the transition from standing or walking to swimming is a logical revolution, which can be described in three ways. First, the unstable surface of the water has been turned into a supporting ground. Second, the relation of consciousness and body has been reverted. Normally, consciousness is on top of the body. In swimming, the body takes the superior position inasmuch as it is the body (not consciousness) that enables us to float in water, and consciousness is reduced to an inferior position of in-ness. Third, it is precisely that part of us that would be the cause of sinking and drowning, namely the physical body with its weight and material substance, that is turned into the very tool for one's floating in the water. Consciousness, the mind, being insubstantial cannot sink, but also does not enable us to float in water.

The patient has to learn how to float and swim in water, in other words, his or her psyche has to let go and entrust itself to the therapeutic process as an objective, apparently autonomous movement. The patient must give up his wish to go through therapy in the upright position, heads up, as standing or walking ego. He or she has to abandon him- or herself, become able to forget him- or herself and all conscious concerns, allowing the process, this unstable, unforeseeable element to become his or her support *and* the stream that forcefully carries the psyche where *it*, the stream, wants. The patient has to allow the images, fantasies and feelings to enwrap consciousness. We can speak here of the submersion of consciousness in the world of *autonomous* images, the stream of *non-ego* images.[38] This stream

---

38 The non-ego, autonomous images must be distinguished from the images, representations, ideas of the conscious mind or ego personality, that is, the person's own concoctions, imaginings, associations. Alchemy distinguished in

is what Jung called the "objective psyche". Where this swimming happens, we have a process that takes place predominantly in the world of the "anima" in contrast to the "animus" and that can also be termed "soul-making" in Hillman's sense. It is the process of an *Er-innerung* (interiorization) or reflection into "the soul."

Just as I previously pointed to the objective structure of therapy and the logical place of the therapist as healing factor prior to any therapeutic actions by the therapist, so I need to emphasize here that not what we *do* or what the patient *does*, but this objective process itself is a most important healing factor. Now the soul's self-regulation can become effective again.

But it is clear that such an interiorization into "the soul" is not suitable and possible in all cases. For example, it would be wrong to expect borderline patients to go this way and to be helped by this way. This is a caution I have to add here. A second point to be made here is that it is of course not enough if the *patient* starts to swim. The *therapist* has to do the same thing. This is why therapy should fundamentally be comprehended as improvisation. Improvisation is the opposite of the application of a technique or of expert knowledge.

As a therapist, in the analytic session, I am *not* present as an expert or specialist. I expect my car mechanic, my dentist, my doctor to be experts in their fields. My *patient* might expect me as analyst to be an expert, too. But I must disappoint that expectation, not because of the lack of the necessary knowledge or skills, but for methodical reasons. To be true to my profession as therapist, I have to let myself fall into the now of this therapeutic situation, e.g., this dream image. And having dropped into the now I am no longer expert. The now is totally fresh, new, unique, and thus it is infinite. If it is really the now into which I have let myself fall I do not come to it all-prepared, but I am surprised by it. I don't come to it with a knowing. And so I have to improvise, pull something out of a hat. This "hat" is myself, my personality, me as the person that I happen to be. I am called to the front, have to show presence; I have to show who I am, what is in me.

---

this sense the *imaginatio vera* from the *imaginatio phantastica* (see Jung, *CW* 12 § 360). Henry Corbin, coming from Islamic philosophy, also sharply distinguished the *imaginatio vera* (imaginations that stem from the realm of *the imaginal* as a reality *sui generis*) from personal fantasies, which are mere subjective fictions.

(See above, Chapters II and III). *Ars requirit totum hominem*, the alchemists said.

The expert focuses on what is called a *problem*, and a problem is a phenomenon that *logically* has been totally encircled by expert knowledge and will be tackled, if not 'attacked', with the help of this knowledge. The now, by contrast, surrounds *me*. After all, I have let myself fall *into* it. For the therapist the dream image or a difficult therapeutic situation is never a "problem" in the sense just given. The expert can and even must leave his subjectivity out; it will be circumvented because his mode is the application of his expert knowledge and skill, acquired during his studies, to the problem. In therapy the therapeutic expert applies the on principle abstract theory established by the psychological school he belongs to, the theory that he brings to the consulting room prior to having started to work in it, rather than applying *himself*. The expert is thus in a way merely the mediator between the given body of knowledge and the particular problem at hand, between the already available answers provided by the psycho-analytic theory to the new questions raised now by the concrete psychological phenomena. I as true therapist, however, cannot leave myself out. I always have to give *my* answer. I have to apply myself to the situation, not my knowledge, because my personality, I as human being, *am* the only real therapeutic tool. To modify here a quotation from Jung from another context[39]: Whether my answer is correct and a good answer or not is not the question. The question is, is it *my* answer, *my* best understanding as the response of the *homo totus*.

Just as I am not the expert who *applies* his knowledge or his theories and techniques, so the patient is, contrary to the customary jargon, not a *case*. A case is always something that is so conceived that it is a particularity that *falls under* a species or universal concept. The species or universal concepts that we are above all dealing with in psychotherapy is the diagnoses. These are all abstractions, sterile constructs up in the air, which are projected upon patients, which in turn means that the patients are subsumed under them. Jung wrote once clearly, and, from a

---

39 I am referring to the statement in the "Prologue" to *Memories Dreams Reflections* (p. 3): "I can ... only 'tell stories.' Whether or not the stories are 'true' is not the problem. The only question is whether what I tell is *my* fable, *my* truth."

psychological point of view, admirably: "I forbid myself thinking in statistical numbers because it impairs your judgment. I treat every case as individually as possible, as the solution is only possible in individual cases and never through general laws and methods." (*Letters 2*, p. 455, to Carol Jeffrey, 18 June 1958). And concerning diagnoses *in psychotherapy* in particular, we have a longer fundamental statement by Jung:

> ... the diagnosis is a highly irrelevant affair since, apart from affixing a more or less lucky label to a neurotic[40] condition, nothing is gained by it, least of all as regards prognosis and therapy. In flagrant contrast to the rest of medicine, where a definite diagnosis is often, as it were, logically followed by a specific therapy and a more or less certain prognosis, the diagnosis of any particular psychoneurosis means, at most, that some form of psychotherapy is indicated. As to the prognosis, this is in the highest degree independent of the diagnosis. Nor should we gloss over the fact that the classification of the neuroses is very unsatisfactory, and that for this reason alone a specific diagnosis seldom means anything real. In general, it is enough to diagnose a "psychoneurosis" as distinct from some organic disturbance—the word means no more than that. I have in the course of years accustomed myself wholly to disregard the diagnosing of specific neuroses, and I have sometimes found myself in a quandary when some word-addict urged me to hand him a specific diagnosis. The Greco-Latin compounds needed for this still seem to have a not inconsiderable market value and are occasionally indispensable for that reason.
>
> The sonorous diagnosis of neuroses *secundum ordinem* is just a façade; it is not the psychotherapist's real diagnosis. His establishment of certain facts might conceivably be called "diagnosis," though it is psychological rather than medical in character. ... The point is, we are not dealing with clinical diseases but with psychological ones. ... (*CW* 16 § 195 f.)

The psychological facts "are far more likely to be concealed than revealed by the clinical picture" (*ibid.* § 196), and "clinical diagnosis is, for his [the psychotherapist's] purpose, well-neigh meaningless" (§ 198). For the truly psychological stance, the patient is an individual with his uniqueness and singularity. To this only needs to be added that the diagnoses of the DSM IV (DSM-5) or ICD-10 are totally medical, abstract, and mindless, which obviously does not detract at all from their considerable

---

40 Here, by the way, we have a very clear example that shows how Jung often uses "neurotic" in a lump-sum, completely unspecific sense as simply referring to psychological disorders in general. Accordingly, a few lines later in the same quote we see that "psychoneurosis" is Jung's generic term for any disorder that *is not* an "organic disturbance".

market value even among psychotherapists.

Having said that a truly psychological approach sees the patient as unique, singular individual[41], which was a point Jung made often (see, for example, above his insistence on "our most private and most subjective life" *CW* 10 § 315), I think we even need to go beyond Jung's insistence on the personality as a totality (which is also an abstraction), and say that a *psycho*therapist needs to focus on the Now: this concrete concern or situation, this complex, dream, topic that has here and now become present in the consulting room. Eachness!

To have to improvise in therapy does, however, not mean that I can go to be a therapist just the way I was born or come from the street, without any knowledge and training. The improvisation should be done by a *practiced, trained* mind. It is certainly the responsibility of the therapist to acquire as much expert knowledge and skills as possible. But to drop into the now means to reduce this knowledge to *sublated* knowledge, to a sublated moment of myself, so that my knowledge is not technically applied to the topic at hand under circumvention of myself as subjectivity, but can enter only under the condition that it has passed through *me*, become embodied in the *real* me, my realness, the *homo totus* that I am and thus has ceased being an abstract theory. Or, with the logic at work in Plato's idea of *anámnêsis* in mind, we can say that our theories and expert knowledge come into play at all only under the condition that our theoretical knowledge acquired in "pre-existence" (that is, prior to having entered the therapy room today) must have been completely forgotten and thus be laboriously freshly rediscovered in the psychological matter at hand that the patient presented us with here and now. As we already heard from Jung: "'Learn as much as you can about symbols and forget it all when you are analysing a dream.'" (*CW* 18 § 483)

Very often the swimming in the stream has to be begun by the therapist. At least in the West it has been my experience that many patients are far away from this kind of swimming. And so I often find it necessary when a patient shows a rather ego and

---

41 All psychotherapists, I assume, would *say* that the patient is a unique individual, too. But typically the psychotherapeutic thinking is nonetheless informed by the medical, clinical mode, and proceeds in terms of "cases" and "diagnosis".

rigidly reality-oriented approach, for example, to dreams, that in how I react to the dream I start to do the swimming in his or her stead, in the hope that they will slowly be *infected* and feel *invited* and *seduced* by the example given to get themselves into the swimming mode. I want to create this kind of an atmosphere. But ideally, and later on hopefully in reality, the swimming should be a mutual undertaking.

This releasing oneself to the process cannot be without a sense of eachness, *Jeweiligkeit*. I have to say to this moment now, to this particular image here, to my dream from last night, to today's sandplay picture, to this present life-situation: This is it! This is what counts! Nothing else exists now, only this. To abandon oneself to the therapeutic process requires that one gives up the interest in having an overview of the process as a whole. I don't need a map, indeed, should not want to have a map. I don't need to understand the process. The wish for a map, for seeing and understanding the way and the stages of the process implies that one wants to take an abstract position high above the process and to look down upon it from outside. On the contrary, I have to leave the process to its own devices and give myself over exclusively to the now. I am *in* the process to the extent that I am submerged in the Now, because the process *is* nothing else but *the self-movement of the Now.* The process continues if the Now changes, and the Now changes to the extent that it has been done justice to, fulfilled, exhausted. There is a dialectic here. The process is alive the more I do not care about the process but only about the Now. My job is to wholeheartedly, with the heat of my passion, dedicate myself to the Now, and it is the job of "the soul" to take care of the movement, development.

So this means that one should not try to cling to what has been in the previous session or sessions. Let it go. Forget it.[42] Ideally one should not put what happened in a session into writing. This writing of a report on each session comes from the wish for ego control. Therapeutically it is counter-productive. No documentation. If you want to document your cases, this shows that you don't trust the process and do not entrust yourself to it. Ideally there should not be case reports and case studies.[43] Case studies

---

42 Wilfred Bion also advocated that one starts every therapy session afresh, without memory.

43 The only excuse for them is the training of the mind sort of in dry dock. But

help to get you out of the process of the Now. Once you put the hand to the plough, you should not look back. You don't have to remember the previous session, *if* it does not stay in your memory of its own accord. "The soul" is the unity of Mnemosyne and Lesmosyne, remembering and forgetting. Our forgetting can be just as important as our remembering. Forgetting is not just a mishap, a deficiency, but psychologically seen it is productive, a production by the soul, as James Hillman pointed out. You might say: But what about continuity? Sure, continuity is important. But the continuity should not be the ego's abstract concept of a continuous development, not the line that could be drawn on a map, but the continuity of my giving myself over to the Now which in turn will guarantee the continuity of the process. And the locus of continuity is not ourselves, our mental understanding, but reality, the real life of the soul, the process itself.

The methodological maxim of a therapy that centers around the releasing oneself to the self-movement of "the soul" was expressed by Jung with respect to the fantasy-image in the following way: "Above all, don't let anything from outside, that does not belong, get into it, for the fantasy-image has 'everything it needs' within itself" (*CW* 14 § 749, I have already quoted this statement above). Expanding on this we could say: the Now, whatever it might be, has everything it needs within itself. This means that the Now is not the abstract now, the point (or short stretch) on the time line. I said that one should not try to hold on to the previous session. We should not mind if we forget what was in the previous session or forget certain details from the biography of the patient or what earlier dreams he or she had. Now we get the explanation for this. If it is the *Now* that has everything *it* needs within it, then this means that *it* brings along with it the memory of those things that are important to it. The true psychological locus of memory is not the ego, but the Now. The Now has to remember, *not I*. And only if the memory indeed comes from within the Now, from within *this* dream, from within *this* problem that the patient just talked about, is it a psychologically relevant memory and not a fundamentally *extraneous*

---

dry docks exist only for the purpose of leaving them completely behind and entrusting one's ship to the sea.

association or abstract interpretation.

America used to be called the melting pot, because people from all parts of the world went to live there and the national, ethnic characteristics with which they came were so to speak melted down so that they could become real *Americans*.[44] I want to apply this image to the idea of eachness, *Jeweiligkeit*, and say: the Now is the melting pot. Whatever in the way of memories, knowledge, ideas we bring along into the therapy session or to this dream 'from home', that is, from ego-consciousness, has to have been melted down in the Now to have either been forgotten or have been reborn from within the Now. The now is now the melting pot and the *vas*.

If therapy is this type of therapy, then something Jung once wrote in a letter applies to it (*Letters 2* p. 583, to Smith 16.VIII.60): "The best the analyst can do is not to disturb the natural evolution of this process. My so-called views about it are only poor means of representing the very mysterious process of transformation in the form of words, which serve no other purpose than to describe its nature." Another quotation from a letter of his comes to mind here once more (*Letters 2* to Vijayatunga, VIII.57 p. 386): "Over against our consciousness we must learn to live as it were unconsciously..." This last quotation has certainly to be taken with a grain of salt. I am not so sure that it would be a good idea for us modern people to *live* as it were unconsciously. But for the kind of therapy I have been describing here this makes a lot of sense. To serve the process as it were unconsciously would simply mean to give oneself over to each Now. It would not mean to give up consciousness or one's intellect.

It would be a misunderstanding that such a statement as that of Jung's—"The best the analyst can do is not to disturb the natural evolution of this process"—might be meant by me as a panacea, a universal remedy. There are

---

44 Unfortunately, America during the last several decades seems to have given up this idea of being a melting pot, instead allowing and fostering, if not on principle insisting on, diversity of ethnic identities, parallelism of different languages, and paying attention to group-specific sensitivities. Psychologically, this is the ego's resistance to the necessity and task of real adaptation.

therapies or therapeutic situations that call for a much more active role of the therapist. I am especially thinking in this context about the importance of strong emotions to be shown by the analyst towards the patient. It can at times in special situations be necessary to get directly angry, even furious at the patient, because only the *heat* of a passionate emotion gets through to this particular patient in his particular situation. Or, it may be necessary and helpful to emotionally enter the therapy situation with one's own joy or excitement about a dream that the patient had and that does not speak to him much, and so on. But such cases do not belong under the heading of *this* chapter.

I thus agree with Jung when he stated (*MDR* p. 142): "... the demand is often made that the doctor or psychotherapist should 'go along' with the patient and his affects. I don't consider that to be always the right course. Sometimes the active intervention on the part of the doctor is required."

Sometimes! But when, and when not? A well-grounded decision about this question requires a differentiated feeling function, a deep, quasi "instinctual" psychological sensibility, psychological tact, and what Jung once called "subtler intelligence" (*Letters 2*, p.410, to Kling, 14 January 1958) and "*intelligence du cœur*" (*CW* 8 § 543).

Excursus on the therapeutic setting and on transference

In releasing oneself to the movement of "the soul", the transference relationship that was already touched upon in the first section of this chapter on one's entrusting oneself to another person is of course deepened, indeed, it is interiorized into itself. Here it comes home to itself. So it might be a good idea to discuss the differences between the Freudian and the Jungian therapeutic *settings* and what advantages or disadvantages each one has as seen from this point in our discussion.

The orthodox Freudian setting is characterized by the fact that the patient is lying on the couch, the therapist is sitting; the therapist can see the patient, the patient cannot see the therapist, since he or she is sitting behind the patient's back. It is obvious that this setting expresses the psychological difference as well as the avertedness character that in turn express themselves in the asymmetrical relation between patient and therapist. The fact that the analyst is not visible for the patient is conducive to the free flow of fantasies and associations. The invisible analyst turns into an ideal projection screen for transference fantasies.

The Jungian setting, by contrast, does not express the psychological difference. Both therapist and patient sit face to face and, so far at least, the impression is created of a symmetrical relation between equals. This has the effect that the analyst is to a much higher degree present to the patient's mind as the real, empirical human being that he or she is, in his or her concrete humanness. In addition, the Jungian analyst has generally a much more carefree attitude concerning his or her own utterances in therapy, is much more liberal in his or her communications. The analyst is not restricted to a few well-considered interventions and interpretations. Naturally, such essential differences in the setting have different consequences. What are these consequences and how are they to be seen psychologically? Especially we have to ask if, because of the fact that the Jungian setting does not express the psychological difference, this difference is neutralized or even totally neglected?

In the Freudian setting the psychological difference is concretely enacted, visibly presented. This means that it is acted out and thus positivized. The difference is distributed upon the two real persons. The analysand, in this setting, represents the only *empirically real* person, while the analyst who is physically present, but sitting invisibly behind the patient *literally* represents a mystery. In other words, the patient represents the *empirical-factual* aspect of the psychological difference, the analyst embodies, or is the placeholder for, the *soul aspect*, its invisibility and fantastic or imaginal character. The *dialectic* of this setting is that the level of the soul's mystery, because it is concretistically represented by the real, empirical person of the analyst, is automatically concretized, becomes *necessarily personalistic*. The mystery being projected upon the analyst *known* to be an empirically real human being in factual reality becomes itself empirical (an empirical "mystery"), and, conversely, the empirical analyst as the real person that he is is subject to the *mystifications* by the patient's transference fantasies. It is thus the logic of this setting that the very invisibility or avertedness, that is, the negativity of the soul aspect is projected upon the realistic level, the personal level: my fantasies about my invisible *real* analyst back there (whom I, after all, know to be factually present and to be an ordinary human being, despite his being invisible behind my back = being mysterious). Such a mystery that has become personalistic and empiricistic is the merely *fantastic*, which now takes the place of the absolute negativity of the soul. The fact that Freudian psychoanalysis focuses on "object relations" is a logical consequence of this setting (or, the other way around, this setting a consequence of "object relations").

So while this setting allows the patient *empirically* to release himself into the infinite openness of the transference fantasies and the endless chain of signifiers, it *logically* confines the fantasies by funneling them into the personalistic framework. So the empirical releasing oneself into free association is not accompanied by an equivalent logical release. Releasing oneself is here an empirical behavior, a literal praxis (the technique of free association), but the logical framework for exercising this praxis is a priori set and closed: object relations. "The soul" is not allowed to *logically* leave the solid ground of reality and to jump into its native element, the fluidity of water. The setting absorbs the invisibility character of "the soul" into *itself* and thus takes care of it once and for all *on the empirical-practical level*; it acts as a *phármakos* (scapegoat) that *disposes* of the logical soul level (and of the psychological difference) *by acting* it *out* empirically. Thereby the therapeutic situation and the process are both *relieved* from themselves having to logically enter the sphere of the mysteriousness of "the soul," and *prevented* from logically entering it. The mystery can here remain merely semantic (the fantastic transference imaginings) or practical-technical (the setting). It cannot become syntactical. This means that the level of ordinary empirical reality is never transcended in favor of the level of "soul" *as* a logically or syntactically *other* level *in its own right*. The logic of consciousness or, as one could also say, one's world view does not suffer a rupture.

Now let us look at the Jungian setting. Here the patient has the analyst before his or her eyes. The analyst is seen as the real person that he is, in his concrete human-all-too-humanness. The setting retains the level of ordinary reality and normal human relations between people as equals. There is nothing mysterious in the form of the setting. This is the one side of the story. The other side is that despite the normality in the external (literal) structure (syntax) of the setting, the actual relation between the two persons is nevertheless characterized by the essential asymmetry between patient and analyst as described above. So the situation is here an in itself contradictory one. The visible setting contradicts the actual logic of the situation. In the form of this contradiction, the psychological difference is *really* present (present in a psychological way). The psychological difference is interiorized, no longer an external technical constellation or behavior.

Precisely because the personal level is not loaded with the mystery (the persons are "*only* that!"), the realm of the actual mystery can open up. If the difference is literally acted out, it paradoxically (or dialectically) gets leveled down, because the mysterious side is not left really mysterious, i.e., logically or syntactically mysterious, but is concretized as a (fantasized or downright fantastic) empirical behavior or fact. Then both sides appear syntactically on the same level, that of external reality. The difference is reduced to a difference in position on the same plane, whereas as psychological difference it is the syntactical difference between two different *levels* or as a real otherness. It is similar to how in modern religious studies the difference between the mythic or divine sphere, on the one hand, and the empirical human sphere, on the other hand, is leveled because the former gods have become semanticized as *ideas* of gods. The mythic or religious ideas are, to be sure, ideas *of* something irrational, not empirical-factual, but these ideas themselves are just as much empirical facts as what is rational. The contradiction has become defused. Only if the contradiction between the two levels is endured can the psychological difference become psychologically real: vaporized, distilled, logical.

Because in the Jungian setting the patient has the analyst as the real empirical person right before his or her eyes and yet develops possibly fantastic transference fantasies, the figure of the analyst becomes *in itself different*, contradictory. There is the fantasy, *and* there is the real analyst. Within the analyst, the difference between him or her as real and as not real is opened up. The fantasy cannot mean the empirical or literal analyst, because one sees him or her in his or her ordinariness. And yet the fantasy is powerful, utterly real, it cannot be wiped away, and it *really* refers to the analyst. The experience of the patient is thus forced beyond the empirical level to another, invisible, intangible level as the true locus of the transference fantasy: the level of the objective, autonomous soul, we could also say, the level of the *interiority* of soul, the level of the images and the image-process as something in its own right.

In this way the psychological process comes home to itself. The transference fantasy comes into its own. I as patient release myself truly and fully to the self-movement of "the soul" because this releasing is not merely *my* subjective behavior, but also objectively what happens to the image process itself: it is *logically, theoretically* released, let free, let go off, so that it can *be* what *it* wants to be. It is not locked into the limits of common-sense reality, not held down to the level of personalistic interaction and "object relations". It is not tied back to the analyst or any other empirical reality, whereby the empirical would become mystified. We could also say the transference fantasy ceases to be positive, positivized, and becomes logically negative. One's full releasing oneself into the self-movement of "the soul" also requires the release of the objective process as such into the negativity of the logical life of "the soul". This is why Jungian psychology does not need the term object relations. The place of the objects is taken by the great diversity of all that is psychological non-I, that is to say, the process of the images, the logical movement of "the soul".

So far I only showed how the analyst becomes in himself or herself contradictory. But the same applies to the patient, too. The patient will in the course of the process experience himself or herself as the existing psychological difference, as the contradiction between himself or herself *and* what he or she is not.

This is why Jung in his *The Psychology of the Transference* described the transference situation in therapy in the form of a quaternio:

This diagram is, of course, burdened with Jung's countersexual anima/animus theory and, as a visualization, is too spatial and schematic to be an adequate representation of the psychological difference. Nevertheless, it does give a first impression of the psychological difference and the complexity of the resulting transference relations. The situation has become much more complicated, the elements have been doubled or quadrupled. But qua schematic diagram it entails the danger of seducing us into literalizing, reifying, and hypostatizing it. But *there are not really four*. Anima and animus are not existing beings. There are only the two people. Anima and animus are in this diagram the expression of the psychological difference, that is, of the fact that the two real persons are not limited to what they positive-factually are (biological organisms, real people, civilian man), but are also an inner infinity and, furthermore, that they also experience themselves as self-contradiction. If they do not apperceive themselves from outside (like two different entities or things in space), but rather interiorize themselves into their true nature, release themselves into the logical interiority as which they exist, then they become apparent to be in themselves the psychological difference, namely, to be at once I and not I. If in therapy they then relate to each other as such, in their internal contradictoriness, this will make the relation rather complex.

The entire coniunctio process, too, as described by Jung by means of the *Rosarium* text, has to be logically released, let go off. We must not project it upon the real patient and ourselves as therapists, stuff it into the patient and ourselves as real persons. In other words, we must not confuse ourselves and the patient with the *rex* and the *regina* of that model. Rex and regina must be let go of. They must not be reduced to mere allegories of the real analyst and patient on the personalistic level, and we conversely must not dress ourselves in the archetypal-numinous garment of these images. The coniunctio, the transference in the Jungian sense, is not an interpersonal relation, not a human interaction concerning what in modernity is called intersubjectivity. Rather,

70

the two real persons in therapy are merely the sign, or empirical underpinning, for an essentially *remote* psychological *background process* that is precisely not *our* feeling or experience, not *our* relating. It is logically negative and takes place *in Mercurio*, in the objective logic of "the soul". It can *be* only to the extent that I give up the attempt to pin it down to the empirical level of my person and the other person, and to the extent that I do not want to be more than just myself, this real empirical human being ("only that!").

These thoughts can serve as a kind of touchstone or *Scheidewasser* (acid test) for the question of whether one has access to truly psychological thinking or not.

The same is true about a criticism expressed by Jung of the figure of Faust concerning the way Faust behaves in the Paris-Helena scene. Jung says: "To the medieval alchemist this episode would have represented the mysterious coniunctio of Sol and Luna *in the retort* [...]; but modern man, disguised in the figure of Faust, [...] *putting himself in the place of* Paris or Sol, takes possession of Helen or Luna, his inner, feminine counterpart. Thus *the actually objective process* of the union becomes the *subjective* experience of the artifex [...]. *Instead of recognizing it, he himself becomes a figure of drama.* Faust's subjective interference has the disadvantage of missing the actual goal of the process, namely the production of the incorruptible substance. [...] a reason for the psychologist to criticize Faust [...]" (*CW* 12 § 558, my emphases, transl. modif.).

The interiority that is meant in our context has nothing to do with introspection. In introspection I take myself as empirical person and existent entity or substance and look at the image process as modifications of this substance (myself, my inner condition). The belief in my positivity, my *Vorhandenheit*, remains the unshaken ground of introspection. Rather, the 'releasing oneself' that is demanded here is one's release into the negativity of Being. It is "the soul's" move from ontology to logic, *logos, Geist*—to the mercurial. Only if the notion of the existent entity, of one's own positivity, is left behind has the real psychological interiority been reached. This is the world of the soul, the world of images. However, images not as ontologized (reified), not as *the* archetypes, *the* imaginal, and certainly not in the sense of the imagination as a psychic function in addition to feeling, thinking, but the world of images as non-being, negativity, as abyss (*Abgrund*, as the mystics said). Ultimately to learn to swim means that I *as* a real, empirical being learn to be *as* non-being, to release myself into the abyss of the logical life of "the soul."

Excursus on releasing oneself into the negativity of the image process and modern consciousness

Only man, as that being that by nature has consciousness,[45] can release himself into his being as non-being, into logical negativity. This capability is due to man's knowledge of his death. The knowledge of death is the entrance gate to soul. Soul, the soul's logical life, the realm of absolute negativity, is the gift of (the consciousness of) death. Just as man's by nature having consciousness makes it possible for him to release himself into logical negativity, so conversely, the human necessity to release oneself into one's being as non-being is nothing else but one's being *conscious* being: *Bewußt-Sein*. The animal, the plant, the stone, they simply *are*. They have a priori been released into their *being* and thus cannot release themselves from it and into non-being. They are identical with their being, and totally obedient to it. But man, to be fully human, must get a distance to his being. In order to get this distance, he must first have *expressly*, *explicitly* gained himself as being, as positivity. One can only get a distance to something and take leave from it, push off from it, if it is something that one has truly made one's own. But here we have to become aware of a difference, a difference between two cultural stages.

Depending on at which stage the therapeutic process takes place, it can go on with or without consciousness. The word consciousness is here used in the narrower sense, as explicit, reflecting consciousness (so to speak as an animus function). Consciousness in the wider sense, man's being conscious-being, is, by contrast, presupposed throughout.

If we take for example the ritualistic masked dance in ancient

---

45 Consciousness in the sense of more than awareness.

societies,[46] we have a case of a releasing oneself into the negativity of "the soul" without (explicit) consciousness. The masked dancer becomes the daimon, spirit, god and has ceased being the ordinary human being in daily life he was before. It is a simple self-abandon, the movement sometimes even into literal ecstasy. The negativity becomes empirical and positive. There is no contradiction since the new state has become possible only because, and to the extent that, the former ordinary state *has been left*. The psychological difference is acted out, not as in the Freudian setting by being distributed upon two people, but by being distributed upon two temporally different states. So here we are in a pure anima world. Similarly in sandplay therapy with children. It takes place without consciousness. The child is given over to the play and oblivious to the world. Also, dreaming is usually, though not always, without consciousness: one is literally asleep and oblivious of oneself. Or we could think of the healing methods of shamans or witch doctors: the persons to be healed allow themselves to be completely drawn into the magical, trance-like goings-on and the *suggestive power* of their mystery. There is no critical distance, no accompanying consciousness that would reflect upon what is going on. Rather, consciousness anima-like simply and wholeheartedly goes along with, allows itself to be carried by, the ritual process, which thus proceeds as an absolutely ego-syntonic one. The I is seduced into to soul world. This is indeed the prerequisite for the healing on this level, just as it is the prerequisite for the effect of rituals in general. This kind of healing is *literally, explicitly* ritualistic.[47] We are in the sphere of *participation mystique* and of the "sympathetic world-relation."

Modern psychotherapy, by contrast, is as a rule based on the existence of a duality; anima world and animus sphere have separated. The innocence of the ritualistic world is lost. This is reflected in the therapeutic vis-à-vis in analysis as well as in the importance of interpretation and reflection of the material that

---

46 I devoted a little paper to the masked dance: W.G., "The Lesson of the Mask", in: *idem, The Neurosis of Psychology. Primary Papers towards a Critical Psychology. CEP* 1, New Orleans, LA (Spring Journal Books) 2005, pp. 257–263.

47 Which must be distinguished from what has been said above about psychotherapy as a ritual. Therapy *appears* as a modern rational undertaking, to some extent even as based on scientific thought.

has come up. There is the clear difference between the text of the dream and the work upon it. The analyst is not like the shaman someone who seduces consciousness to be enwrapped by the magic of a ritualistic procedure, but wants to make conscious, conscious even of the meaning of the autonomous image process aimed at in a Jungian therapy. At times he even needs to confront the patient directly, emotionally, and sometimes even vehemently so, quite apart from the fact that analysis in general has the purpose of confronting the patient inexorably with his truth. Its ultimate purpose is truth, insight.[48]

If at this level or status of consciousness it is a case of releasing oneself to the self-movement of "the soul" and its image process, then it is indispensable that consciousness is precisely *held on to*. In our case even our diving into the image world is marked by a rupture, a rift. For if we were to follow the image process in this new situation *without* consciousness, the result would be consciousness's cocoonment in its own contents (Jung: "consciousness's becoming unconscious", *CW* 12 § 563, transl. modif.), or, in worse cases, an inflation of consciousness or even delusion. The duality of the modern world must here be expressly endured. We stand *vis-à-vis* our dream images. We think *about* the images, ask what they *mean*. Consciousness is retained. As Jung said, modern man wants to know, wants to understand. I would add: qua modern man he *must* want to know, because he is consciousness in the narrower sense and thus cannot let himself be totally drawn in, with the same innocence as during previous ages. The child or the primitive or the religious believer never asks for the meaning of a ritual. The goings-on are their own fulfillment for them.

The psychological difference therefore has intensified. Under the conditions of adulthood in our modern situation, our releasing ourselves into the soul's self-movement, of which we have spoken, can no longer have the form of a completely ego-syntonic oneness. No trance, no enchantment, no simple believing. All this would be irresponsible for modern man. Our releasing ourselves must have the form of a *conscious* abandon, one that is accompanied by the

---

48 Jung accordingly ended his 1912 essay, "New Paths in Psychology", with the sentence: "*Magna est vis veritatis et praevalebit*" (Great is the power of truth and it shall prevail, *CW* 7 § 441), probably citing Tertullian, *Adversus Praxean* 26. He could also have quoted John 8:32: "Truth shall make you free".

knowledge about our giving ourselves over and ipso facto stays aware of our subjectivity (our being subjects who experience imaginal contents as their object of consciousness). So it needs our bridging the gap between the two demands. We have to learn to endure the difference, to encompass the two, and thus advance to the identity of difference and identity.

However, even today there is sometimes the possibility that adults go without consciousness through a therapeutic process, e.g., in sandplay or as a process of painted or dreamed images, so that healing takes place precisely without consciousness. In such cases modernity, if it had already been reached in the first place, is *temporarily suspended*. Modern consciousness takes *time out*. The therapeutic process in such cases proceeds mostly unconsciously, subliminally, below the threshold of that consciousness that keeps existing above it. We could say that the process goes on subterraneously, literally subconsciously. Everyday-consciousness does not take part in it; it passes over it. The therapeutic process has thus a similar status as our nightly dreaming that is essential even if it does not become conscious. Or it is similar to a geological phenomenon like the Danube Sinkhole (the disappearance of the Danube river into an underground riverbed and its reappearance far away). After the therapy session, the patient returns to his normal modern everyday world, as if there had not been a therapy session at all. But this kind of therapy is a special case. One could call this special case "day dreaming" or "waking dreaming" in the literal sense, not to be confused with what usually is meant by these words (the reverie, our conscious fantasizing). In this type of therapy the patient sort of sleepwalks through therapy, and here it is especially important what Jung said, namely "not to disturb the natural evolution of this process."

There is, however, a great difference to real sleepwalking: because the therapist is present. Normal sleepwalking is done in the solitude of the individual self. The presence of the analyst shows that the duality is not totally left behind. The rupture of modern reflecting consciousness makes itself felt even here. The psychological difference is here distributed upon two persons: The analyst in this constellation represents the continuity of the reflecting consciousness, which in such cases relieves the patient from the task of retaining, for the duration of the session, his own consciousness to which he or she will return after the session. This makes once more obvious the fact that we are dealing here with a temporary suspension of consciousness and that this subconsciousness of the process despite appearances stays contained *within* the brokenness of modern consciousness.

3. Releasing one's illness from one's subjectivity into an objective Universal

Now we come to a very different healing effect of psychotherapy. In most therapies the patient is in the course of time automatically trained to think in terms of the theory of the respective school of psychology; in a Freudian analysis, he or she learns to interpret himself or herself, e.g., in terms of the family romance, of the Oedipus complex, the transference significance of *all* images and of all behavior, etc., or, in a traditional, orthodox Jungian analysis, he learns to comprehend himself in terms of the shadow, anima and animus, the Self, the healing power of symbols, myths and fairytales, of the archetypes and the numinous, etc.

The healing effect of this development must not be under-estimated. Here we have to keep in mind what psychological illnesses are. To be sure, they are first of all a certain, e.g., neurotic, borderline, or whatever structure. But in addition they are also the fact that this structure is *enclosed* and *locked* within the singular individual, locked to such an extent that they are inaccessible even to the I of the individual. His illness is usually an absolute riddle for the patient. If now in therapy the patient learns in detail that and how the personal symptoms and mechanisms of his illness are all known, understood, and explained by the particular psychological *theory*, something opens up. What up to then had been only *in* the patient slowly turns into the patient's being *within* this theory, being a particular "case" of this or that (part of this) theory. A fundamental reversal. His or her singular afflictions are now being attached to, even getting *sublated* in, something larger, something universal and spiritual or intellectual. What had been merely subjective, now has received an objective reality transcending my own subjectivity.

76

This does in no way alter the neurotic structure itself; *it* is not healed; the illness stays. But for the suffering individual this change has an important healing effect in so far as it frees him or her, as the singular personality that they are, from being *the exclusive locus* of the illness. The illness can be released from within its enclosure in the personality into something larger and not-subjective, the psychological doctrine, and released from the status in which it compulsively had to be literally, existentially, sometimes even physically, *lived* and *embodied*, to a level that *belongs to the mind.* It has become something that can now be thought, imagined, comprehended. This move concerning the illness from fact to mind is a radical psychological transformation (reminiscent of the move from fact to speech, language discussed above in connection with the topic of "confession"). It does by no means merely bring a subjective *feeling* of relief; it also objectively, factually relieves the personality from the burden of having to harbor its neurosis within itself. It opens the box.

* * *

So far so good. But this important psychological move of releasing the illness as fact into theory often overturns into the opposite of a release. In many therapies the patient is cocooned into the theory of the respective school of psychology. Not infrequently therapy amounts to a veritable brainwashing. Under the *title* of "making conscious" a making *unconscious* is thus going on, because the patient is lulled into the doctrine of the respective school. Releasing oneself now means having become absorbed by the impressive suggestive power of the theory or technique as well as by the mystique that the therapist creates around his theory or technique. You then finally leave therapy *believing* in "the unconscious", in the family romance, or in Mandalas, symbols and archetypes or in the good and the bad breast or in the interactional field, etc. Here what Sonu Shamdasani once pointed out comes to mind:

> If there is one thing that psychology and psychotherapy have demonstrated in the twentieth century, it is the malleability of individuals, who have been willing to adopt psychological concepts to view their lives (and that of others), in terms of a play of conditioned reflexes, a desire to kill one's father and sleep with one's mother, a psychomachia between the good and the bad breast, a parade of

dissociated alters, a quest for self-actualization through peak experiences or contorted twists through the hoola hoops of the symbolic, imaginary, and the real."[49]

Psychological theory turns into ideology, a creed, a belief-system. The patient learns *officially* to think neurotically and to take the neurotic thinking as a special truth. Psychologically, logically, the individual cedes his metaphysical (not his empirical-practical) responsibility to the higher authority of the given doctrine; subjectively, this is a blissful relief. Through his belief the patient is partially freed from his suffering.

Just as I had to emphasize earlier that one therapeutic factor is the quiet, motionless structure or logic and syntax of the institution of therapy as such, prior to any particular therapeutic interventions by the analyst in the consulting room, so I must here stress that the relief is not due to the truth or correctness of this particular theory, but to the *fact that* it is a doctrine, an abstract universal that from now on has to shoulder the metaphysical responsibility for oneself. This type of *displacement* from patient (person, human soul) to abstract theory through a kind of "brainwashing" is very common in psychotherapy. It is also a great temptation (how wonderful to stylize a therapeutic process as an individuation process in Jung's high sense!), but of course not commendable.

I stated a while ago that the release of one's illness into the status of an objective intellectual reality transcending my own subjectivity in no way alters the neurotic structure itself; *it* is not healed; the illness stays.

Here I want to remind you of Jung's insight, which he exemplified only with respect to Freud, that psychological theory can in itself be structurally neurotic. This is indeed a most important insight. And although Jung did not see this, it applies to some extent to his theory, too. This is not the place to show this in detail. One simple hint must suffice: by thinking in terms of

---

49 Sonu Shamdasani, *Jung and the Making of Modern Psychology*, Cambridge (Cambridge University Press) 2003, p. 11. Jung expressed much the same idea with respect to one particular theory, briefly named by him the infantilism theory, by pointing out that "there are numberless patients who ... are at bottom only too ready to subscribe to the infantilism theory, because it offers them the possibility to pass off the irritating 'infantile elements' as a 'nothing but'. And in many cases this theory offers a heaven-sent way out of the unpleasantly acute problems of real life ..." (*CW* § 348, transl. modif.).

the opposition of consciousness and "the unconscious", depth-psychology ontologizes or hypostatizes the neurotic dissociation and thus does exactly what is one of the problems in neurosis. Conventional psychology as practiced by analysts all over the place is usually not the *healthy* thinking vis-à-vis neurotic thinking, but merely raises *in the patient* what is going on in neurosis to the level of theory.

But this raising the neurosis to the level of theory is precisely what has a healing effect. The healing effect of therapy here is that the personal neurosis *as* neurotic structure is *displaced* from the individual into the abstract Universal of the psychological theory or practice. This goes beyond our earlier discussion of the transposition of the illness from fact to mind, which was a truly psychological change. Now we are concerned with a different aspect. In shamanism the shaman took the illness of the patient upon and into himself in order to overcome it within himself. In psychotherapy, something similar happens, only that here it is the general theory or practice that happens to function as the equivalent of the shaman. It absorbs the neurotic structure into itself, thereby relieving the patient from having to carry or embody it. The only, but crucial difference to shamanism is that the psychological theory or practice does not resolve the illness, here the neurotic structure, but rather ennobles it by ontologizing it. Thus the healing effect that this possible aspect of therapy has is that, while the therapist believes that through each of his interpretations and his lifting repressions he is resolving the *neurosis*, he—completely unintentionally, unwittingly, maybe even *malgré lui*—merely is one by one transferring, loading, it upon a *phármakos*, a scape-goat: the objective structure of his psychoanalytic theory.

The mode of believing in the different elements of the respective psychological theories (I mentioned the family romance or the belief in Mandalas, symbols and archetypes or in the good and the bad breast or in the interactional field) amounts to a freezing, fixating, positivizing. The notion of believing is traditionally associated with the image of the rock on which one has built one's house. The theory becomes the rock, and this rock is not, like the alchemical lapis, fluid, mercurial, the *aqua permanens* or *vinum ardens*, but rather what is called a scientific truth. The fact that both Freudian psychoanalysis and Jungian analytical psychology, although in different ways, attempt to present themselves as *science*, in other words, present their findings as positive facts, facilitates this hardening. Releasing oneself or one's illness upon a rock is not a real releasing. It is more like a leap from a precarious, insecure situation into a much larger, firm safety net, a leap through which the personality holds onto itself as something solid. A real self-release would require that that into which one releases oneself has also *in itself* been released from its positivity as a substance and into the fluidity of the logical movement and absolute negativity of "the soul." And it would mean that through it that which released itself would itself become fluid, mercurial.

One of the main criticisms that Jung raised against Freud was that Freud had raised his method to a theory. But at times and in certain ways Jung did the same thing in his own way and with his different material. Jung made out of his experiences a theory, "liquid lava" or "magma" froze into stone, as he indicated. Or at least this is what happened to his thinking in the hands of the Jungians. They solidified it into a kind of doctrine to be mechanically applied to psychic phenomena. Psychologically it is, however, essential that one's ideas are kept in the status of a mere method, a *mode* of approaching phenomena, that they stay *performative* and do not become ontologized. Often Jung himself was very much aware of this and clearly expressed himself accordingly. Thus he once said, to mention only a few meager examples, "Scientific theories are merely suggestions how things might be viewed" (*CW* 4 § 241, transl. modif., in the German original, the whole sentence is italicized), and, completely in contrast to any focus on a translation of the patient's psychic phenomena into his theory, "My aim is to bring about a psychic state in which my patient begins to experiment with his own nature—a state of fluidity, change, and growth where nothing is eternally fixed and hopelessly petrified" (*CW* 16 § 99). Not the interpretation of the neurosis, but the patient's own experimenting with himself!

* * *

A particular danger in traditional Jungian therapy is that the attempt can be made to simulate or imitate the special case we discussed earlier, the case of a temporary suspension of consciousness so that the movement of "the soul" or the image process can go on subterraneously beneath the threshold of consciousness. Thus it is, for example, possible that in a therapy the patient is helped to *stylize* himself or herself *as if* he or she could still enter such an authentic subterraneous process although for this patient, as a thoroughly modern person, this is no longer possible. Then one pretends an innocence and naivety that is not really there, a pseudo-innocence. It is the ego-steered *simulation* of an underground movement, a conscious process of pretending to be unconscious. One cocoons oneself in symbols, in mythic meaning. The result is a kind of psycho-kitsch, a mystification. Banal personalistic emotions and interpersonal reactions—ego affairs—are then often dressed in a transpersonal, numinous, mythic garment. The notion of my real mother, e.g., is, just like that, blown up into the mother archetype. Jung warned against the theosophists' posing as an Indian potentate (*Theaterkönig, CW* 9i § 28). In the same way we now have to warn against posing as the *Rosarium* figures of *rex* and *regina* and all kinds of other archetypal figures. This kind of phenomenon has a religious prehistory. During the 19th century, Gottfried Keller, a Swiss poet from Zurich, e.g., unmasked and criticized the analogue of such behavior in his novellas under the title of sanctimoniousness (*Frömmelei*), while a century earlier something similar was criticized under the name of *Schwärmerei* (rapturous enthusiasm), e.g., by Kant.

Obviously this kind of thing has a great fascination for some people; there is something seductive about it, and judging from the books they write, some Jungians seem to try to satisfy the need of the public for this kind of cocooning oneself in mythic meaning, thereby acting as the Pied Piper of Hamelin (*der Rattenfänger von Hameln*). For, this image comes to mind here because the Pied Piper seduced the children of this town with his flute to follow him. Here in Jungianism, too, it is mainly the *musical quality* of the numinous and archetypal that is cultivated in such quarters. The specific intellectual content remains diffuse and, above all, it is arbitrary, exchangeable. It does not really matter *which* archetype or myth or fairytale is experienced, the only thing that matters is the enveloping numinous or mythical aura evoked by it or projected upon it in order to rock

81

consciousness to sleep with and to befuddle oneself. This is Richard Wagner transferred from Bayreuth and from literal music and literal theater to the consulting room.

In a very different connection, concerning a particular Christian idea by way of example (namely, the idea of redemption "through the blood of our Lord Jesus Christ"), Jung once strictly warned that by piously repeating such formulae, one slides back into the past with them, is being made unconscious again, and that this is so because one does not intellectually *know* what these words mean. Instead of *thinking* them one abandons oneself to the emotional impression they make, and the impression they make is that they "sound so solemn and so beautifully like Sunday and so religious, so splendidly religious".[50] It is patent that the same applies, in the case of modern patients, to all mythological symbols, mandalas, and archetypal ideas. They can be made to sound so splendidly sacred, if one confines oneself to, and wants to indulge in, their emotional impressions.

4. Releasing oneself into *oneself*, into one's being or nature

We talked about releasing *something*, certain contents (one's secret feelings or thoughts), and about releasing *oneself*. And we talked about releasing oneself to another person, the therapist, and releasing oneself to the soul process and the Now. Now we come to a very different type of releasing oneself, namely one's releasing to or rather into oneself. We could also say that it is our releasing ourselves *from* our imprisonment in our subjectivity. Jung wanted that we learn to face ourselves objectively, see ourselves from outside, as an objective vis-à-vis. I have to become an other for myself, that is to say, I have to take myself as an objective fact. Jung bemoaned the "childlike naïveté" of modern man, saying: "He has no objectivity toward himself and cannot yet regard himself as a phenomenon which he finds in existence and with which, for better or worse, he is identical" (*MDR* p. 341).

This getting an objective distance to oneself is not easy. To begin with, we are enclosed within our own subjectivity. We see

---

50 C.G. Jung, *Über Gefühle und den Schatten*. Winterthurer Fragestunden. Textbuch, Zürich and Düsseldorf 1999, p. 22. My translation.

ourselves only subjectively, in terms of our self-image, our ego-ideal and our demands upon ourselves. Many, many people condemn themselves or feel guilty or ashamed because they are not the way they think they ought to be. This is an indication of their exclusively subjective relation to themselves and their being totally *identified* with themselves. They think their being or nature should follow their subjective thoughts and wishes (which, paradoxically, often are modeled after general moral principles or the values of one's social environment, which shows that our subjectivity is by no means isolated, solely-subjective, but from the outset socially constructed). They think that *they* should be able to decide how they are. Their guilt feelings or shame are evidence of the fact that they do see that *in fact* they cannot decree or dictate how they are, but that they hold on to this idea nevertheless. It is not dethroned, not decomposed. In the guilt feeling or shame the illusion is celebrated that they ought to model themselves according to their own or society's standards.

So to become objective to oneself, the task would be to release oneself from one's subjective self-definition, one's ideals of and demands on oneself. I have to let myself *be* the way I am. I am not my own maker, my own architect or designer. I am not my own idea, my own fantasy, which I can shape the way I want. Rather, I *find* myself as a given hard fact. Long before I came up with my ideas of how I should be or wish to be or think to be, I was already finished, an accomplished fact: biologically determined, socially imprinted, and formed by my own history, my own earlier and now habitual responses to the world. I exist in the perfect tense. My nature precedes myself. I come too late with my wishes and demands. This is why we must diagnose as neurotic the deep, painful feeling met in many people that actually they ought to be different, that only if it were (morally, socially) permitted to be the way they are only then they would be allowed to be the way they actually are. Permission or prohibition make sense only with respect to something still pending. But the decision about our particular nature has already been made. The way we are lies behind us, in the perfect tense.

So all there is to it is an *unconditional surrender*. I have to come down from the height of my imagined sovereignty with respect to myself (i.e., to my actual makeup) and humble myself. I have to bow *under* myself, *under* the natural *fact* that I am, *under* my immutable nature. I have to learn to *receive* myself the way that I am given to myself by life or nature. I am now subject, subjected, *to* myself, under myself. I as modern subject am only the keeper or custodian of myself. My nature has been entrusted to myself like a ward. Formerly, under different world conditions, this attitude was expressed and actually *lived* through the idea that one is a Creature of God.

This also means that I have to learn to take a strictly empirical, almost scientific, attitude towards myself. This is the place where Jung's above-cited dictum about his aim "to bring about a psychic state in which my patient begins to experiment with his own nature" belongs. To find out who I really am I have to expose myself to tests by real life situations and see what their result is. Jung at the same time also described the condition aspired to as a "state of fluidity, change, and growth where nothing is eternally fixed and hopelessly petrified". In the present context, we could translate this as a condition in which the patient has left his fixed ideas of his self-identity behind, which are illusionary. This is so because we do not come into the world with a manual that gives a full description of ourselves. I do not start out with an a priori knowledge of myself. Rather, slowly, very slowly, piece by piece, over the course of my life, and often painfully, I have to *find out* from experience how I really am; because initially, my real being is inevitably enveloped in my ideas, wishes and illusions about myself so that I don't see it.

Secondly, after having got to know how I am, I have to learn to be obedient to my being-so *as my law*. The animal, as Jung once said, "is a well-behaved citizen in nature, it is pious, it follows the path with great regularity ... Only man is extravagant ...".[51] Animals are law-abiding. They are born into their law; they exist, as it were, as their perfect tense from the outset. Thus they cannot have any illusions about themselves, they cannot deviate from their law. But what animals are by birth, we humans, whose distinction it is to be logically exiled from our *being*, evicted from the perfect tense that we are, and released into the realm of ideas and fancies, we have to acquire in our self-relation and through a conscious ethical achievement. It is the achievement of our

---

51 C.G. Jung, *Visions: Notes of the Seminar given 1930-1934*, ed. Claire Douglas, 2 vols., Bollingen Series, Princeton Univ. Press, 1997, p. 168.

submitting to our particular nature, of allowing our perfect tense to catch up with us, nay, overtake us. Only then have we come home to ourselves and settled in our being. It is part of human existence as *human* existence to live with or *as* a hysteron-proteron.

We could describe this shift to my receiving myself from life the way I am also in sexual images. This would make the shift one from "engendering", "fathering" myself to the "conception" of myself, i.e., my self-conception, where conception is of course diametrically opposed to the other sense of the word: idea, view, design or blueprint. It implies, on the contrary: I am pregnant with myself as the hard fact that I am, and during my lifetime I slowly have to give birth to myself.[52] We could also say that it is a move from *deontology* (from Greek *tò déon*: duty, obligation, what ought to be) to ontology (from Greek *tò ón*: what *is*). With a still other image we could say: My nature has been entrusted to me like a ward. I am no more than the caretaker, custodian, of myself.

To really humble oneself *under* one's own nature would mean not only to endure, put up with, to take care of, oneself the way one happens to be, but also to truly *make peace* with one's own nature, to *forgive* oneself one's deficiencies and weaknesses, to *allow* oneself to be the way one in fact is, and even to *befriend* oneself as this real person *with* all these deficiencies. Only with the *undiminished solidarity* with how one really is has one really let go of oneself and has the arrogant idea been fully given up that one could demand of oneself to be a certain way. Before I said that I exist in the perfect tense. Here, now, we could add that precisely in my factual nature *with* all my deficiencies I have my real perfection and accomplishment (in contrast to the illusionary, inflated, grandiose idea of perfection produced by wishful thinking). I *am* already perfect.

Even my own past, my own deeds in the past, I must let alone. I must not permit myself to have guilt feelings on account of my own deeds. Guilt exists for the purpose of being *consciously acknowledged* (known) and *borne*. Not for feeling and thus indulging in them.

---

52 This is why the end of life was in Greek called *teleutê* (completion, fulfillment). The word *frühvollendet* in German means 'early deceased', but literally 'early fulfilled, completed'.

Jung once stated (MDR p. 325): "The greatest limitation for man is the 'self'; it is manifested in the experience: 'I am *only* that!'"

Sometimes, psychotherapy is understood as self-development, and self-development is taken to mean self-improvement. In our context, we must see through the goal of self-improvement as illusionary. Therapy does not make us better—unless one means by better more truthful and simple. It can only *reduce* us to what we really are, by abrading *omnes superfluitates*, as alchemy put it, all stuff and nonsense in which to begin with we might find ourselves unwittingly enwrapped, unwittingly because we mistook this "stuff and nonsense" as our true identity and essence.

Earlier we discovered that consciousness is only fulfilled when it is self-consciousness, where we have an I that is We and a We that is I. Now we discover something analogous. Subjectivity is only fulfilled subjectivity when it has released itself from its own dictate and has become objective to itself. Only if I have let myself fall into the insight that "I am *only* that!" and that "I am *immutably* only that" have I become truly subjective. My subjectivity is not itself subjective, but in itself an objective fact. I am not the supreme ruler of myself (of my real nature), but the subject under the supreme rule of my nature. Subjectivity is in itself dialectical, it has its own other *within* itself.

To release oneself into oneself may sound like a one-time task and something global: I release myself into my nature. But my nature is not one entity, thing-like, a whole, indivisible. Rather, my nature consists of thousands of individual, often tiny, feelings, emotions, desires, reactions, impulses, thoughts, prejudices, intuitions, etc., which change during my lifetime. So this submission under oneself is a permanent ongoing task. I have to let myself fall into each individual momentary facet of myself. Here we need the notion of eachness and nowness, *Jeweiligkeit*.

This notion implies also a temporal sense of my having to release myself from my self-definition or from my expectations concerning myself: I do not have to be the same today as I was yesterday. I do not have to hold on to opinions, standpoints, decisions, likings just because yesterday I held or expressed them.[53] My needs and views may have become different, and so to release myself into myself also implies releasing myself into my *now* being-so, i.e., my being-so as a living, changing process. As I said, I have to have an empirical attitude towards myself and experience in each situation anew how I am, or rather find myself to be. I have to release my nature into its contingency, into my being my own *Zu-fall*, ac-cident,[54] for indeed my being-so befalls me, falls to my own lot. There has to be room also for the surprise that all of a sudden I discover different reactions and feelings in me than I was used to hitherto. So the perfect tense of my nature can also be a future perfect.

There is a German saying: *die Katze aus dem Sack lassen*, lit. to let the cat out of the bag = to let the truth come out. My nature is the cat. I must let it out of the bag of my preconceived ideas about myself and let it run where *it* wants to run. Here again Jung's word comes to mind about the patient's having to begin to experiment with his own nature and about his reaching a state of fluidity where nothing is once and for all fixed and hopelessly petrified. I have to give up control over my nature. My nature is not *my property*. It is an Other to me, a vis-à-vis. My nature is, to use Jung's example of the bank employee who shows a friend *his* bank, the *bank* whose employee I am. Or it is a cat with its own will, and ultimately an untameable one. The image of the cat that I let run where *it* wants shows the inner dialectic of the perfect tense of my nature: my perfect tense is an open future, it will only emerge in the course of my life *as a whole* and will itself have only become perfect, *vollendet*, fulfilled, with my death, its *teleuté*. In biology or medicine, what one puts under the microscope is called a slide preparation. Some patients come into the consulting room, and many people live life, as such slide preparations, in other words, already *präpariert*, stylized as a specimen. This is putting the cat into the bag. And there are many bags, bags provided by one's family, society, various groups one belongs to, one's church and even oneself.

To let the cat out of the bag does not mean to live irresponsibly. For example, it also means to *expose* one's real being to the relentless criticism from the people one lives with and to face up

---

53 Cf. the humorous Swabian sentence: *Was kümmert mich mei Geschwätz von gestern.*

54 Heidegger's word *Zu-fall* is often translated as *be-falling*.

to this criticism, even to accept and bear it, provided it is justified; and even if it is not justified to bear without grudge the fact that this is what others think about oneself; this is objectively my place in my relations to others. But of course often the criticism is justified. And to really let the cat out of the bag means to live with and hold one's place in the knowledge that there is something about oneself that indeed deserves criticism. This, by the way, is what is meant by Jung when he speaks of the integration of the shadow.[55] But it has also a lot to do with what is called character, strength of character. Character shows when I in view of what deserves criticism do not stab myself in the back, do not betray myself, do not end the wholehearted solidarity with myself. I have to stand by myself precisely when the going gets tough. No guilt feelings. No feeling of shame. They are the most common form of a self-betrayal, the form in which I become what Nietzsche called the "pale criminal."[56]

In a deeper sense, letting the cat run free does not mean living irresponsibly because I will discover that this cat, too, is herself a "law-abiding citizen". In my true nature there is a firm sense of right and wrong and a sense of responsibility. And it is precisely the other way around, namely, that irresponsible behavior comes about because the inner morality of our true nature is covered by the ego's selfishness, by all sorts of ideological excuses, or by temptations leading one astray.

By letting myself be the way I am, I release myself from the (illusionary) *ontological* responsibility for myself, that I initially thought to have and that had inflated me into partially confusing myself with the creator-god. If anyone, then only God has to take the ontological responsibility for my being-so. But, on the other hand, by (logically, psychologically) receiving my nature as given to me and unconditionally surrendering to it, I accept the *empirical, pragmatic* responsibility for myself, for what I do with my nature, with my gifts as well as with my faults and weaknesses. And I accept that not God or life or whoever else, but *I* have to *pay the price for my being-so*, for the real empirical consequences that my being-so has.

---

55   Often the shadow concept is abused in terms of a self-correction, self-improvement program.

56   Fr. Nietzsche, *Also sprach Zarathustra*, "Die Reden Zarathustras", in: *Werke in drei Bänden*, ed. K. Schlechta, vol. 2, p. 303.

That I am subject (subjected) *to* myself and the guardian or advocate of my real being-so (however my being-so may be at a given time), also means that I am given to myself as an assignment. My being-so is assigned to me as a task, and it *needs* me. My impulses, my feeling, my thinking need me as their mouthpiece and advocate, their representative; they are dependent on me, because only through me can they become real and come into the world, receive an existence in the world. I have to put all my strength, the strength of my whole personality, behind my being in order to put my entire heart into giving reality to its mere potentiality. My being and all my essential emotions, wills and thoughts are, so to speak, like the shield of a fighter in battles of old, the shield that is only of use to the extent that the fighter stands behind it with all his strength to withstand the impact of the next spear or sword stroke. I must stand up for my nature, take responsibility for it.

So I exist twice. I am this twofoldness of I as the contentwise completely indeterminate, abstract strength of personality, *and* I am the many specific determinations of my being, which by themselves, without my standing up for them, are weak and helpless. The strength and weakness at issue here are logical (not biological or psychic) strength and weakness. It is only a matter of one's courage not to hide, the courage not to abandon and betray the impulses. The real, practical strength of the personality as a character is precisely not a given, always already existing, possession, a kind of innate endowment, but it is *the result and product* of courage. The strength only comes into being when I energetically put myself behind my being and fill it with all the might of my being, and a character comes into being when I do this regularly.

We probably need to go a little further. Standing up for me ultimately also means the readiness even to impose myself with my being-so on my fellow human beings. In the last analysis, what is at stake with all this is my psychological becoming real, coming down to this Earth. At first we are unreal, we are just floating in the clouds, our real being and essence, our nature, belongs psychologically only to the realm of mere potentiality, even if biologically or psychically it is always already real. But that is not enough. Psychologically, my ideas, opinions, feelings, peculiarities only become real when I acknowledge them.

Whoever waits for permission to be allowed to be as he is, decides to remain in the realm of mere possibility. He is like the man from the country in Kafka's "Before the Law", who also does not have the courage to enter into reality. The reason for this is not only the fear of others, but much more profoundly the narcissistic self-infatuation, the insistence on preserving one's immediate unity with oneself. One does not want to step out of oneself and thus become another for oneself. One avoids the transition from One to Two. Permission to be as I really am would relieve me of losing the unity with myself, namely of experiencing me as a duality, indeed a discrepancy between myself and the nature given to me and of taking it upon myself.

Of course, the fact of my standing by my own being-so (in its eachness) and of my imposing myself on others with it, does not give me carte blanche to simply act out these impulses, etc. I am not advocating antinomianism and libertinism here. By taking myself as I am, I release myself from my ontological or logical responsibility for myself. But by in this way also *receiving* myself as I am, I assume the empirical, pragmatic responsibility for myself. The point is not to live it out, but to show oneself with one's own peculiarities, with one's weaknesses, with one's perhaps differing opinions, and then to endure without grumbling any criticism, attacks, loss of love, disregard. It is precisely the reaction of others that belongs to my becoming real, because it is psychological, human becoming real and soul and being human are only possible in the human community in which I live. And insofar as the community does not only exist outside of me, but is also already at work within me, "to release oneself into one's own being" also means to place oneself unconditionally under the unsparing judgment of self-criticism.

Releasing myself into myself has consequences beyond my self-relation. Or rather, since consciousness is an I that is We, and a We that is I, this releasing immediately includes my relation to other people. I will have to release them, too, into *their* being-so. I have to take them the way *they* are, with a passive-receptive and empiricist rather than a dictatorial attitude. Here, too, I have to wait and see how they in fact are, and not imprison them in my expectations, presuppositions, ideals, and demands. I have to learn to see the members of my family, my friends and all the people that I have to deal with in my professional or private life as *hard facts* and unconditionally surrender to the perfect tense of their factualness, their being-so.

So many patients approach others by logically locating them in the "future tense", with an "they ought to", as if the other people were still unformed and malleable by our wishes. Psychologically or logically, I have to grant to everybody *"the right"* to have faults, to be stupid, even malicious, as well as to dislike or hate me. In other words, with respect to the nature of my fellow human beings I also have to let the cat out of the bag and let it run the way and where *it* wants.[57] Which does not mean that empirically-practically I could not protect or defend myself. It is just like with the weather. Each day I have to look out the window and see how today's weather actually is and have to take it the way it is. But taking it the way it is does not imply that on a rainy day I could not take a rain coat and umbrella to protect myself from the rain. Logically, I have to take people the way they are; empirically-practically I can protect myself and my interest, and of course I will be able to do so all the better the more I have logically simply accepted their being-so as a fact that is not worth getting worked up about instead of getting stuck in resentments or emotions like anger. My reaction to such disappointments from others must be forgiveness and renunciation.[58] Stefan George's *"Drum lernt' ich traurig den Verzicht ..."* (Thus I sadly learned renunciation ...), although spoken in a completely different context and with a different intent, is very appropriate here. I must make my peace with the people.

There is a quotation in Jung where this attitude of releasing another person, in this case one's mother, into her factualness occurs; Jung wrote: "a sensible person [*ein Wissender*] cannot in all fairness load that enormous burden of meaning, respon-sibility, duty, heaven and hell, on to the shoulders of one frail and

---

57 Gotthold Ephraim Lessing: *"Was dir ziemt / zu tun, ziemt mir, erst zu vernehmen, nicht / vorauszusetzen."* [With respect to what it is *your* duty to do, it is *my* duty to first hear or learn (i.e., to wait and see if you have done it), not to anticipate and presuppose it.] (*Nathan der Weise*, Vierter Aufzug).

58 With forgiveness and renunciation I am not talking about one's *behavioral* response. I am speaking on the psychological or logical level.

fallible human being—so deserving of love, indulgence, understanding, and forgiveness—who was our mother" (*CW* 9i § 172).

Jung speaks of indulgence, understanding, and forgiveness. Of course, we must here keep in mind the difference between the psychological (or logical, metaphysical) level and the pragmatic level. It is only on the psychological level that I have to grant everyone the right to be evil and to be against me, and to bear this, to allow him to do so without grumbling, while I can naturally defend myself pragmatically, that is, in empirical behavior. Logically: unconditional surrender, empirically: "why smitest thou me?"

This releasing others into the factualness of their being and letting the cat out of the bag even with respect to them has also a reverse. Often patients feel guilty saying or thinking something negative about their parents, or even they do not dare to do so at all. They feel they have to protect them. They still keep them psychologically under their wings. This means those patients cannot release their parents *from* the bag of their (the patients') subjective ideas, wishes and demands and cannot release them *into* their objectivity and factualness. But to let the cat out of the bag also means to call a spade a spade. At least to myself and to my analyst I have to be able to admit frankly, and without glossing over the situation or making excuses for them, that, e.g., my mother or my father was nasty, cruel, violent or whatever, *if* that was my experience.

Often one is prevented from simply being honest about such things because one feels it would be a lack of filial piety or be presumptuous to say such bad things point-blank. But psychologically, it is precisely presumptuous not to say it. One is not humble enough to bow underneath the facts. One still wants to exercise control over the truth.

Another frequent escape from this necessity is to say that this is only one's subjective view of things that maybe is not objectively correct and so one should not say anything bad about others as long as it is not proven. But this is cowardice, a defense mechanism. In therapy in particular, but also in life at large, we are *only* concerned with a persons's (the patient's) subjective experience, his or her subjective truth. All views are subjective. There is nothing else. Naturally, I can only say what *I* feel, believe, or experienced. What else? The point here is to own up to one's own real impressions, feelings, experiences, regardless of whether they could stand up in a courtroom or not, that is to say, to own up to one's *subjectivity*, one's "being *only* that!". Whether they are absolutely correct or appearances is not the question. The only question is: is it *my* honest impression, *my* best knowledge. As I said earlier it is my very subjectivity that has to become objective to myself.

There is an important Letter to the Editor by James Hillman to *Spring Journal 65*, 2000, pp. 1–4 ("Sometimes a Cigar is just a Cigar"), illustrating this calling a spade a spade with respect to the behavior and character of a well known Jungian, C. A. Meier.

Whether it is in the direction of forgiveness or in that of condemnation, ultimately it is the same kind of freeing other persons from the obligation to be immediately identical with their notion (their office, job, duty, obligation). It is the opening up of the difference between the ideal and the real.

There is another area to which this kind of releasing applies. The one is the nature of the world, of the social conditions one lives in, or of life in general. These I *psychologically* (not always practically) also have to allow to be the way they are. I don't need to make a fuss over every little thing. I don't have to run up to and wallow in every pile of manure I see and then complain about the stench and dirt. I can pass by. Not even because of the injustice, imperfection of the world in general and all the misery that exists in it, do I have to make a fuss inwardly. Here, too, it is important to be "a sensible person", *ein Wissender*, in the sense of Jung's word about one's attitude towards one's mother. In Western thinking, the problem of a *theodicy* played an important role, the question of how the idea of the goodness and justice of God can be reconciled with the observable facts of evil and suffering in the world. If one releases the world or life into the factualness of its being, this question disappears.

The releasing oneself into one's nature is very different from one's releasing oneself to the process of images of "the soul." Here it is no longer a question of learning to swim in the waters of the soul. Rather, what we have here is the topic of the full development of one's own subjectivity, it is about becoming self, becoming I in the full sense. For I am only subject in the sense of modern subjectivity to the extent that I have become the subject (one who is placed under the authority of someone or something, *Untertan*) *of* my being and an *objective other* to myself. It is the move of growing up into psychological adulthood, the move out of the naive, childlike idea that one's being would have to be modeled after one's wishes and ideals, the move out of the status of mere potentiality into reality and out of the "future tense" into the "perfect tense". The child *essentially* lives in the psychological status of the future, in the mode of wishing, hoping, imagining. Not so the real adult. He or she is an adult because he or she has *logically* or *psychologically* left the future behind, has stepped out into *objectivity*, or from potentiality into reality. The future has been reduced to a mere sublated moment within the perfect tense. The adult has outgrown the future (i.e., wishful thinking). Thus the adult is a *grown, staid* man, a *grown, staid* woman (*ein gestandener Mann, eine gestandene Frau*). Because the grown up person has the future logically behind himself, he or she is *psychologically* free to *empirically-practically* plan for the future, take concrete precautions and is often overcome by worries about the future. All that is unknown to the child.

But worrying about the future is the sign of a still incomplete growing up because it betrays the ego wish to control the future. The full self-release into oneself can also let go of the possible course of events and receptively let the events come the way they are and have to be. The full self-release has thus released the person into the *simplicity of being*.

5. Releasing oneself into one's *pathology*, and the *notion* of oneself into the notion

The term neurosis can have two very different senses in Jung's writings, quite apart from the fact that it can also be used in a narrow, specific sense as well as in a wider more general sense that comprises all sorts of psychic disorders. The difference I have in mind is one that concerns the psychological appreciation of neurosis, the evaluation of it.

■ The one sense of neurosis is entirely negative. A neurosis is really sick and needs to be ruthlessly overcome. This sense is

94

best exemplified in Jung's description of his own childhood neurosis at age 11 and how he overcame it (*MDR* pp. 30 ff.).[59] It was characterized above all by fainting fits whenever he had to go to school or do his homework. The turning point to the cure was what Jung expressed with this favorite phrase of his, "the collision with reality" (p. 31). We need not be concerned with the details of what happened. Essential for us is two things. First, he fought it consistently with sheer will-power. Whenever a fainting attack wanted to come, he reacted with a general moral exhortation, "Damn it, one doesn't have fainting fits!" (my transl.) and forced himself to study. Within a short time, this symptom was in this way radically overcome. The second crucial aspect is his insight ("That taught me what a neurosis is", my transl.), namely, that it was solely due to a "whole bag of tricks"; "I myself had arranged this whole disgraceful situation", "the whole affair was a diabolical plot on my part", a cause of feeling ashamed (p. 32). We see, neurosis in this sense has no redeeming value. Its diabolical plot needs to be eradicated.

■ The other sense of neurosis is that, as despicable as it may appear, it nevertheless has for Jung psychologically an intrinsic value, "for hidden in the neurosis is in reality a piece of still undeveloped personality, a precious piece of soul ...", which means that one's being rid of one's neurosis "would not be a cure, but an amputation". "A psychology of neurosis that sees only the negative aspects empties out the baby with the bath-water ..." (*CW* 10 § 355, transl. modif.). "It [the neurosis] is not what is cured, it cures us" (§ 361, transl. modif. Jung italicized this whole sentence). "... it is precisely in his neurosis that the values which the individual lacks are to be found" (*CW* 7 § 93, transl. modif.). What manifests in this understanding of neurosis is "an urge [*Trieb*] towards self-realization". "We could also speak of a retarded maturation of the personality" (*CW* 7 § 291).

Obviously the two notions of neurosis are strictly opposite. They exclude each other. According to the *second* view, Jung's

59 I discussed this extensively in my book *Der Jungsche Begriff der Neurose*, Frankfurt/M, Berlin, Bern, New York, Paris, Wien (Peter Lang), 1999.

own reaction (both practical and theoretical) to his childhood neurosis would not be a cure, but an amputation. Instead it would have been essential for Jung *not* to have tried "to 'get rid' of [his] neurosis, but rather to find out what it means, what it has to teach and what its goal and purpose is" (*CW* 10 § 361, transl. modif.). And conversely, if we were to apply the first view to the second sense of neurosis we would have to criticize the latter sense of it as one's condoning it, one's taking "the neurotic conjecture quite seriously and thus" "be taken in by it" (*CW* 10 § 365, transl. modif.). We would have to see it as one's riding the same hobby-horse as the neurotic (cf. *CW* 10 § 362).

The solution of the problem that consists in these contradictory views concerning neurosis is the insight that what we have here is a case of *equivocation*. The one word neurosis is used for two fundamentally different psychological *phenomena*. The particular type of phenomenon for which I would reserve the word neurosis is a soul situation that has a number of very specific characteristics, the most important one of which is that it is a maneuver or mise-en-scène by the *neurotic* soul (not the ego!) to counterfactually and spitefully establish as present reality and absolute truth a soul truth that is objectively already known to be obsolete and irredeemably lost. Due to its counterfactual nature it cannot change reality as such. It can in empirical reality only produce its fake truth in niches within the prevailing real reality and in the subjective and wretched form of disease, pathology, neurotic symptoms. The soul's spiteful absolute insistence on living and (neurotically) celebrating a lie in an individual is what makes a true neurosis *neurotic*.[60]

The other type of phenomena that in Jung's parlance go also under the name of neurosis is that of a form of disorder that is by no means the result of a "shameful plot", a mise-en-scène, on the part of the soul, nor a neurotic self-contradiction, as in the case of a genuine neurosis. The symptoms or the pathological condition in a genuine neurosis are each an end in themselves; they are performances *by* the soul, demonstrations, the soul's deliberate production and mise-en-scène that has its purpose and

---

60 See my *Neurosis. The Logic of a Metaphysical Illness*, New Orleans, LA (Spring Journal Books) 2013, now London and New York (Routledge) 2020.

fulfillment within itself.[61] The second type of pathological phenomena, by contrast, is productive and innovative. It is the innocent, spontaneous, surprising stirring, and self-manifestation, of the soul itself *under the conditions* of an ego-personality that has become completely identified with one form of itself and is thus too rigid, solidified, encrusted. The piece of soul that shows itself in this way can either be a split-off (repressed) part of the person's personality or one that has never before been connected with his personality and thus is something completely new that manifests for the first time.[62] The more important and interesting case is that of the emergence of a new aspect of the soul.

Jung is aware of the two different senses of "neurosis" or "neurotic", but usually at best hints at it. For example, it is clear that when he mentions that

> If the worst comes to the worst, he [the patient] will even put up with his neurosis, once he has understood the meaning of his illness. More than one patient has admitted to me that he has learned to accept his neurotic symptoms with gratitude,[63] because, like a barometer, they invariably

---

61 Just think of hysteria, compulsions, phobias, anorexia nervosa, etc. This is also why Jung's childhood neurosis can ultimately not serve as a fully authentic example of a genuine neurosis (of a neurosis *sensu strictiori*), despite its "diabolical plot" character. The fainting fits were means to an end, they had their purpose and fulfillment outside of themselves, namely, in Jung's being excused from having to go to school and doing his homework. The reason for its being partially deficient as a case of a genuine neurosis is that the fainting fits had their origin to some extent in the *ego's* intentionality, i.e., in ego wishes or purposes, rather than being solely produced by the autonomous soul. The absolutely compelling power of neurotic symptoms stems from the fact that the ego has no share in them. The ego is in neuroses the powerless victim of the autonomous soul's maneuvers. But because in the case of the boy Jung the ego was complicit in the production of the fainting fits, although not solely responsible for them, it also becomes understandable why Jung could relatively easily and quickly all by himself overcome his childhood neurosis through the efforts of the now *enlightened* ego.

62 *GW* 10 § 364: "... dieses abgespaltene oder nie mit ihm verbundene Stück seiner Persönlichkeit ..." Jung envisions two different possibilities: the part of personality that stirs from within is either a split-off, repressed part or it is something completely new and unexpected that thus tries to emerge for the first time. The *Collected Works* translation—"... that split-off fragment, supposing it were ever part of him?"—misses Jung's point.

63 Cf. *CW* 10 § 361: "We should even learn to be thankful for it ..." Here the reason given for this gratefulness is that neurosis "is nature's attempt to heal him". This is quite astounding in the context of our question, "What heals?",

told him when and where he was straying from his individual path, and also whether he had let important things remain unconscious (*CW* 16 § 11),

he has neurosis as something psychologically productive and helpful in mind—here as an alarm system against the loss of adaptation—, whereas when he states in the same paper, "So long as one is moving in the sphere of genuine neurosis [*im Gebiete der eigentlichen Neurosenpsychologie*] one cannot dispense with the views of either Freud or Adler" (§ 24), he is talking about the first, purely negative sense of neurosis. And in this case he marks it as different from the other constructive sense by adding the qualifying adjective 'genuine' [*eigentlich*]. In general, it is characteristic of Jung's concept of neurosis that there are two opposite senses of it and that according to it it is essential for the therapy of a particular neurotic patient to "decide whether a neurosis should be treated from the infantile angle or from the adaptation angle" (*CW* 10 § 349), where the phrase "infantile angle" refers to the one-sidedly reductive interpretations such as those of Freud and Adler. But what, as far as the terms "infantile" and "adaptation" are concerned, complicates matters is that shortly before, in § 345, Jung had precisely insisted that what is 'infantile' "is something extremely ambiguous", inasmuch as in some cases it might "be more advisable to examine these 'infantile-perverse' fantasies for their creative content than to trace them back to the cradle, and to understand all neuroses more as an attempt at adaptation than as an unsuccessful or otherwise distorted wish-fulfilment".

Conversely, Jung's own childhood neurosis as well as what I call genuine neuroses in sense of my cited book must have to be considered as the result of the soul's refusal to adapt to an altered situation, so that Jung's phrase viewing neurosis "from the adaptation angle" is also ambiguous. It can mean the soul's attempt to create a new "'other' personality" (this is Jung's preferred interest) or, again, viewing a neurosis from the adaptation angle can mean seeing it as the soul's stubborn refusal to accept its own new, already understood truth and its entrenching itself in a fake truth (which would be what makes a neurosis *thoroughly neurotic*).

---

because it means that neurosis itself (understood in the sense indicated) would have to be counted among the major curing factors!

But now I want to continue with the discussion of the logic of the productive, creative form of so-called neurosis. Consciousness has entrenched itself in its attitude. Jung often spoke of one-sidedness. But it is less this obvious one-sidedness that is the deeper psychological problem than the fact that the form (attitude) that is lived by the ego-personality (or ego-consciousness) is, due to the latter's having become totally identified with it, lived mechanically, routinely: sort of automatically, as it were; its life, the animating soul, has gone out of it, with the effect that the form has made itself independent. It has not only become, qua abstract or ossified attitude, something in its own right, but also something for its own sake, indeed, the ruling principle of psychological life.

This is a dissociation. The ego-personality is cut off from its own animating soul. But this dissociation is not a neurotic dissociation, because there is nothing neurotic (in the strict sense) about it. It and its one-sidedness is not the result of a psychic (unconscious) act of splitting-off, of a repression, and is not a mise-en-scène. It is merely the result of an almost normal, slow developmental process of "loss of soul" through continued practice of the same attitude and the ensuing habit-formation, through which consciousness imperceptibly got into a rut and the form or attitude of consciousness took on the character of a routine.

A minor everyday and harmless example of such a soul tendency's or soul truth's spontaneous stirring and asserting itself is what Freud called *Fehlleistungen*, Freudian slips. It is to be assumed that they are often (but not always) of the type of the manifestation of something split-off or repressed, rather than of the other type of the first emergence of a totally new aspect of the soul, that comes to the fore because of the person's finding himself in an altered situation to which he (his consciousness) is ipso facto no longer adapted.[64]

---

64 Adaptation is a crucial concept in Jung's thinking. When he uses it, it is not the external sociological concept of adaptation to the conventions and rules of the society in which one lives. Jung's concept is a psychological one. It refers always to the adaptation to *one's own* situation. Even if an altered situation is an external one (one of the natural or social conditions of life), psychological adaptation means inner, psychological adaptation, namely, that change of the constitution of *consciousness* (its concepts, categories, expectations), through which consciousness, its attitude, becomes psychologically equal to the real

The consequence of the solidification of consciousness's attitude is the loss of flexibility and this, in turn, implies the loss of the capability to adapt to an altered situation. Notwithstanding the partial ossification of the attitude of consciousness, the soul is and remains (logical) *life*. It is dynamic, its self-unfolding in the course of time. In addition to biologically-induced people's growing up and aging, soul ideas, too, go through phases of first immediacy, youthful enthusiasm, critical reflection, slow maturing, and finally decomposing, being superseded. Furthermore, what the soul objectively *produced* in the form of cultural works as well as social institutions, etc., has repercussions for the soul itself. It all of a sudden finds itself in an entirely different situation from that which existed prior to its own productions (just think of today's radical transformation of the world through modern technology). And this new psychological situation—be it induced by biological aging or by the inherent logical process of its own thought or by the exposure to the self-produced transformation of the world in which it lives—requires the soul's adaptation to it. But that soul that as consciousness rigidly identified with its abstract habitual attitude has become dissociated from itself. It has lost the flexibility of attuning itself (that is, its logical form or constitution) to the new situation. It has lost the capability of

---

situation. Whether the person submits to the external conditions or fights them, rebels against them, has nothing to do with it. This is why I find Jung's following distinction between adapting oneself "outwardly to the world and reality" and one's "adapting to the self, to the powers of the soul" (*CW* 10 § 326, transl. modif.) or ("1. Disturbance of adaptation to outer conditions. 2. Disturbance of adaptation to inner conditions" *CW* 18 § 1087) misleading, nay, psychologically downright wrong. It introduces the modern neurotic dissociation between Inner and Outer and suggests two orientations in opposite directions. It suggests that to approach soul one needs to look *inside* ("introspection"). But even my own dreams are never inside me. I see them in front of me. Here it would be better to keep in mind what Jung himself pointed out elsewhere: "When I shift my concept of reality on to the plane of the psyche, where alone it has its legitimate place, this puts an end to the conflict between mind and matter, spirit and nature [and, I add, Inner and Outer], as contradictory explanatory principles. Each becomes a mere designation for the particular source of the psychic contents that crowd into my field of consciousness" (*CW* 8 § 681, transl. modif.). *Mind* and *matter* (both as experiences, contents, objects of consciousness), not Inner vs. Outer. Adaptation is always the same. It is adaptation to whatever content of experience has altered.

simply going along with the objective changes to which it finds itself exposed. Jung's formulation for this psychological state of affairs is that

> ... consciousness is faced with a situation and task to which it is not equal. It does not understand how its world has altered and what attitude it would have to assume in order to be adapted again (*GW* 9/I § 61, my transl.).

This situation might lead to painful frictions or conflicts *between* the ego-personality or ego-consciousness and the world. But such frictions and conflicts would mainly belong to the social and cultural arena and to conscious attempts to resolve the conflicts one way or another. *Psychologically* more important in our context is the fact that a consciousness that is completely identified with, and thus safely encased in, its accustomed abstract form can be undermined by subversive soul activities from within. After all, we are dealing here with a case of dissociation. The living soul was not simply gone, totally eliminated, but the soul as rigid ego-consciousness was merely cut off from itself as living soul. Now the latter stirs again from underneath and makes itself felt in the form of symptoms. In the pathological phenomena that make up a psychological disorder of this type, soul aspects try to force their way into consciousness. The more consciousness is rigidly identified with its present form, the more the soul's stirring from underneath has to become pathological. It is forced into the status of symptom because it cannot fit into consciousness's solidified form. Rather than being repressed, it is here merely excluded. "That thing in you which should live is alone; nobody touches it, nobody knows it, you yourself don't know it; but it keeps stirring, it disturbs you, it makes you restless, and it gives you no peace" (*CW* 18 § 632). It "wants to *mitleben* [to have a share in your life: to become an integral part of your actually lived life and, which is even more important, a part of the self-definition of yourself as a person]" (*Erinn.* p. 331[65]).

The psychological symptoms of that type are therefore more than a reminder. They are in themselves the first immediacy of the new personality, the new attitude, the new constitution of consciousness, that wants to come into being. This is why Jung

---

65 The translation in *MDR* (p. 329: "for it is here to stay") misses the point.

rightly said that it is precisely in them "that the values which the individual lacks are to be found", that they contain a precious piece of soul and thus are not what needs to be cured, but what cures us (where "cure" means the soul's getting once more in accordance with itself and consciousness's getting adapted again, namely to its altered situation). Trying to cure us *of* them, *of* this "precious piece of soul", would indeed amount to an amputation.

Whereas neuroses are characterized by the fact that neurotic dissociation means the fundamental and radical disruption of the soul as self-relation and as self-regulating system, those psychological disorders in which the pathology is the expression of the insistent stirring of the excluded soul that wants to *mitleben* are precisely due to the workings of the fully intact self-regulation of the soul.

This is a fundamental difference. For this reason it is crucial in one's psychological practice to distinguish, in the sense of a clear differential diagnosis, cases of the latter type of symptom from those of the genuinely neurotic type, just as neuroses as *psychological* illnesses (as the soul's own home-made mise-en-scène) need again to be distinguished from merely *psychic* disorders, impairments, defects (those that are simply *causal effects* of bad conditions or experiences in one's biography, above all but not only during early childhood). But as pointed out earlier, it might be more adequate to avoid speaking of "cases" in the sense of the persons who come to psychotherapy. The more appropriate approach would be to see the task of the differential diagnosis as something to be applied to each and every pathological *phenomenon*. It may well be that in one and the same person any combination of (a) neurotic features or even a full-grown neurosis, (b) symptoms that have to be seen in the light of a consciousness cut off from the soul's life, and (c) impairments due to causes can be found, be it simultaneously or surfacing at different times. It is of course imperative for psychotherapy not to fall into the same type of trap as that consciousness that became completely identified with its abstract form by rigidly identifying a real patient with a particular diagnosis, which happens all too often ("she *is* a neurotic", "he *is* a borderline personality", etc.).[66]

---

66 About the problem of diagnoses in psychotherapy see above, Chapter IV.2, p. 59.

For the consciousness that is no longer adapted because its world has changed without consciousness's having been flexible enough to attune to the changes, the soul aspects that try to force their way into consciousness in the form of symptoms are completely ununderstandable. It cannot at all realize that the symptoms contain and bring precisely those *values* that the individual lacks. It sees in the symptoms only something utterly irrational and sick: not only ununderstandable, but also downright meaningless and therefore not even worth attempting to understand them. The soul as solidified, if not ossified, consciousness is, after all, cut off from itself as the living soul.

In addition to their being ununderstandable, they also pose a threat to consciousness. This is so because consciousness is in love with its own values; it treasures them as the highest, absolutely *right* values and thus as irrenunciable and indispensable.

This is the ego view of the symptoms. The psychological view is the opposite, as we know, namely, that they have a message and meaning for the suffering individual, that they bring what he or she lacks and needs, soul truths and values, indeed, the lost *life* of the soul as such.

As far as the ego experience goes, we could compare such symptoms, each of them, to Pandora's box because for the ego they are a box of evils. This is why the lid of the box needs to be kept closed in order to prevent those evils from coming out. The ego's not understanding *is*, as it were, the lid that keeps those evils under control, even if only in the form of quite disturbing symptoms. As myth tells us, Pandora opened her box of evils, and thus they were allowed to spread uncontrolled throughout the world. What before this opening of the box had been a well circumscribed and safely contained content within the box, had now been let loose so that it permeated Being as such and people were exposed to them.

From the psychological point of view the image of Pandora's box can be helpful. The only thing that has to happen is a kind of "revaluation of all values": what is in the box is precisely not evils. Rather, what the box contains are essential and necessary pieces of soul, precious soul truths and soul values. And the opening of the box is not a sorry mistake, due to an ill-advised curiosity, but psychologically indispensable. What is in the box called symptom needs to come out, be let freely loose into the world, so that I find myself *in* it, surrounded by it on all sides, as a *truth*.[67] It now can permeate the logical constitution of consciousness itself as its (the symptom's or soul truth's) Notion, Concept, *Begriff*. This is what would amount to consciousness's new "attitude", as Jung put it, which would allow it to be adapted again.

At the same time, the symptom would have disappeared. It *is* symptom only as long as it has "unopened Pandora's box" character. The moment that what it contains has come out so that consciousness is exposed to it and redefined in its internal logical structure, in other words, the moment that contained content has changed into prevailing, acknowledged, and understood truth or meaning or notion, the form of symptom has dissolved.

A symptom is a soul truth, a notion pressed down into the status of a mere object or content, namely into the status or form of a dumb and blind "fact"—a behavior, a psychic emotion, sometimes even a body phenomenon—so that qua fact it is on principle excluded from consciousness. I said that psychological symptoms (of the non-neurotic type in the specific sense of 'neurotic') are the first immediacy of the new personality. We could also say they are the first immediacy of the living soul trying to force its way into consciousness. But qua symptom, the soul appears in soulless form, positivized, thing-like or as an empirical occurrence. This is exactly what "first immediacy" means. Its soul character, that is, what Jung called its meaning or message and what I call its form of truth or notion, is still packaged and systematically hidden in empirical fact. This is why we assign them to "the unconscious". They are fundamentally, on principle, un-conscious, unthought, in the sense of appearing as something that does not need to be thought or understood.

But comprehended as the soul's first immediacy, the symptom is like a printed and sealed book. Inside, the book may contain poems, novels, or philosophical insights. The book qua book, however, is precisely an empirical thing without meaning, that is to say, a thing that does not *mean*, does not present a message. The poems in the book, by contrast, are not things. They *do* mean, *are* meaning, *are* notional. However, as such *they* exist only in the soul or mind, only when they are read or heard and *consciously*

---

67 Compare this to what was said earlier in Chapter IV, 1 about confession.

received and understood, but not as printed letters. Symptoms thus have for the psychological mind the same logical structure as writing (in contrast to speech, language): the logic of *imprisonment.*

What is psychologically necessary in cases of disorders of this type is that the book is opened and understood, that the positivized signs of "writing" are read, that is, transformed into living speech. What used to be object or thing has to become linguistic, notional: *thought.* This is what alchemy had in mind when it demanded that the spirit Mercurius had to be freed from its imprisonment in matter and when it said: Beware of the physical [we could also say: the literal, the writing, *écriture*] in the material, the prime matter. Don't get stuck in the first-immediacy *form* of sign, book, thing, factual event. From writing to spirit, from thing-like fact to living thought.

I assume that everyone in the Jungian world would agree that symptoms need to be understood, that their meaning and message needs to become conscious. The closed book, which the symptom at first is, must be opened and read. But I also suspect that the cherished project of in this sense making conscious is commonly not comprehended *mercurially* as a move from positive fact or thing to spirit and living thought. Rather, the desired integration into consciousness is quite positivistically imagined (and treated) like the spatial transportation of the book that contains the writing about the meaning from one library in the cellar called "the unconscious" to the other library in an upper storey called "consciousness". The book itself now obviously appears in consciousness. But it is not opened, not read, not understood. The meaning or message remains something thing-like, an object or content of consciousness. Consciousness does not have to think it, not exist as, not *be,* the thinking of it. Mercurius stays imprisoned in the *object* called archetypal meaning, and the psychologist earns his living as a "bookseller". The patient on his part can proudly enjoy the *possession* of his new valuable books and make an emotional fuss about his having found "meaning", having discovered the "god or goddess" in himself or herself, and indulge in the mindless adoration of "the numinous" and "sacred" (which coincides with my earlier point about releasing the patient into the ideology of a particular school of psychology, while leaving the structure of the neurosis intact and not dissolved).

Psychologically or mercurially understood, "making conscious" or "integration into conscious-ness", as actually *reading* the book, would require a move in the opposite direction. Not one's bringing the book up from down there into consciousness, but *my* going under into the book and

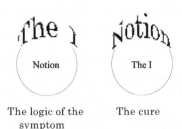

The logic of the symptom

The cure

into what is written in it. Leaving the book metaphor behind and returning to what it referred to, the symptom, we can say that I have to release myself into my symptoms, into my pathology, let myself fall into it, and in this way logically expose myself to it, embed myself in it. Then I am *in* it, surrounded by it. I have settled in the abyss, the logical negativity, of my symptom, and this is what lets *it* open up, lets *it* reveal its meaning or message. This is what "understanding" means.

Only in this way is the symptom on its part released into *itself*, into its notion, its truth. It has come home to itself, has explicitly become what it implicitly had been from the outset, but what had been concealed behind its first-immediacy appearance as empirical thing or fact. Now it has become transformed from fact to speech, notion, and soul, from substance to subjectivity (*my* hearing[68] and "getting" the message), from ontology to logic/*logos*, spirit, living thought. Having become notional it finally can come home to me and penetrate, permeate me. When this is the case, it has become my (new) truth (or one of my truths). Only in this way is it integrated into the logical constitution of my consciousness or, as Jung would have put it, has my attitude become an altered

---

68 True hearing is always an event of one's going under, submitting, one's letting that which is to be heard *surround* oneself. In my book, *Working with Dreams. Initiation into the soul's speaking about itself* (forthcoming), I suggested that analytical psychotherapy should be conceived as a "listening cure", not a "talking cure"! Greg Mogenson had already earlier introduced the phrase "Listening Cure" (in the title of Chapter 5 of his book, *The Dove in the Consulting Room. Hysteria and the Anima in Bollas and Jung*, Hove and New York [Brunner-Routledge] 2003). In talking, the subject that talks keeps itself in the superior position. Talking is always a talking *about* something as the object to be discussed.

one so that consciousness can be adapted again to its altered world.

The relation to one's own pathology proves to be a special case of the release of oneself into oneself and into one's being or nature discussed in the previous section. I have to allow the symptom or its mental content to strike and permeate me. I must let myself fall into the abyss, into the logical negativity, of my symptom and settle down in it. In this sense, Jung was able to say, for example, that where my fear is, there is my path that I must go. "One's anxiety always points out our task." "... the thing we are afraid of involves a task" (*Letters 2*, p. 517, to Victor White, 8. January 1949, resp. p. 509, to Dr. S., 30. September 1948).

Having insisted on the necessity of the I's having to go under into its symptom, I now come to the second aspect of the topic of this section. Here it is imperative to listen to the exact formulation of "logically expose myself to it, embed myself in it". This "logically" means that *I* do not have to embed *myself*, not me in the literalness and positivity of my existence, in my mortal nature. It is not an empirical behavior, nor an *existential* shift. I am already embedded in my pathology as part of my nature. Rather, this embeddedness and exposure is a logical, psychological move. The going under has to happen on the level of my *notion* of myself, my *self-definition*. Releasing myself, letting myself fall really means that my initially prevailing notion of myself as subject and agent who has to perform these tasks gives way so that I am dropped into and land in the notion as which I indeed exist. *I* do not have to change; *my notion* or *notions* have to change. I as individual, existentially, am not the object and focus of therapy. Therapy's aim is not *my* transformation, *my* individuation, *my* becoming self. Soul-making is *psychology-making*, as I explained in *Working with Dreams* (Part III, chapter "psychotherapy—the making of psychology"). the whole existentialist understanding of psychotherapy is due to the personalistic fallacy. It is the modern ego's inflated claim that I myself am the one who is all-important and at the center of therapy. Therapy is therapy of our notions, concepts, dogmas, ideals, our consciousness,[69] not of the person that we are. The person is taboo, must not be touched.

To the extent that what we are concerned with in this section is

---

69   Cf. the important work by David Miller on the idea of the therapy of ideas.

a transformation from the logical status of positivity into that of logical negativity, it could also be discussed in the second part of this paper, the part on therapeutic *work*. For, this transformation is what alchemy tries to attain to under the names of fermenting corruption, sublimation, distillation, evaporation. But as these terms suggest, this kind of work is in itself logically negative work, *recursive* progression, a reflection or interiorizing of the prime matter into its *inner* mercurial essence.

———————————

This concludes my discussion of the various forms of releasing oneself. In each case, to release oneself is the *goal* of therapy, the *method* of therapy, and the *healing factor*, all three at once. The usual separation of goal and method and result cannot be maintained in psychology and psychotherapy. The method is not the *way to* the goal, but in itself the goal. And this goal is at the same time what heals.

V. The therapeutic effect through work on consciousness

Releasing oneself means a passive letting go. Now we come to the opposite attitude, an active doing and one's incisively confronting consciousness. In the beginning of this book I stressed the importance of the *indirectness* of soul work. The work on consciousness that we will now turn to is, however, characterized by a clear directness. Nevertheless, it is not a directness of focus and will aimed at a healing effect. Rather, it is the direct approach to concrete individual psychic phenomena, symptoms, neurotic reactions, today's moods and feelings, the patient's hopes, fears, illusions, his fantasies and dream images; it is the *therapeutês'*, not the healer's, attendance to whatever shows itself in therapy, his simply doing his daily work. The point is psychologically to do justice to the respective phenomenon at hand, without any ulterior motive or ego program.

What needs to be discussed now is thus the work by the therapist on the patient, but one that the patient ideally should slowly take over and continue practicing upon himself. It is the soul's dialogical self-relation that at first is interpersonal, projected upon, distributed between, and acted out by, the two people in the consulting room, but that later on should become integrated into the consciousness of the patient as the soul's internal dialogue with itself.[70] There are again different kinds of work on consciousness.

1. Work on the "resistances" to releasing oneself

I stated that the attitudes that had been discussed under the title of "releasing oneself" and those that will follow under the title of

---

70 According to Plato the soul is a dialogue that the soul engages in with itself (*Sophistes* 263e: ... *entòs tês psychês pròs hautèn diálogos áneu phonês* .... Cf. also *Theaitetos* 189e: *lógon hòn autè pròs hautèn he psychè diexérchetai*).

"work on consciousness" are opposites. But this does not mean that even in the area of "releasing oneself" this active kind of work upon consciousness would be totally excluded. It is always possible to raise the question whether the patient's opening himself to the other person, his releasing himself to the process or to himself and into the symptoms is unreserved enough or whether there are not resistances in the way so that it become necessary precisely to explicitly *work* on the capability to let go.

But what is the spirit of such work? I used just now two terms that are problematic, "confrontation" and "resistances." They might suggest a kind of pressure exerted explicitly, implicitly, or unwittingly upon the consciousness of the patient that he *ought to* give up his resistances and release himself. The pressure is there even if it comes only in the form of the therapist's mere internal *wish* that the resistances might be overcome, a wish nevertheless making itself felt as pressure via the counter-transference. My understanding of therapy is that this kind of pressure is ethically intolerable. I as therapist, I think, have no right to interfere with the core of the personality and subjectivity of the other person, that is to say, with his or her freedom. Any kind of pressure in the sense indicated would be a transgression, a trespassing into the innermost sanctum of the subjectivity of the patient. I have to *respect* the freedom of the other person even to reserve himself, to not open himself, to come to therapy and *yet not* release himself to the relationship and the process. From the bottom of my heart I have to honor this as his legitimate right.[71] Therapy has to be done in the spirit of real freedom, a spirit that is the external and early (preliminary) form of (objective, not subjective-emotional) love.

The word "resistance" *is* the *objectified* moral pressure; and the practice of *Widerstandsanalyse*, analysis of the resistances, is the *institutionalized* moral pressure to overcome the resistances, quite independently of the question whether the analyst

---

71 Cf. Jung: "As a doctor I cannot demand anything of my patients in this respect,... ... I must leave my patient to decide in accordance with his assumptions, his spiritual maturity, his education, origins and temperament ... I cannot presume to pass judgment on his final decisions, because I know from experience that all coercion—be it suggestion, insinuation, or any other method of persuasion—ultimately proves to be nothing but an obstacle to the highest and most decisive experience of all, which is to be alone with his own self ..." (*CW* 12 § 32).

subjectively and actively exerts pressure or not. This is why I strike the term resistances from my psychological vocabulary as a technical term. (I might still use it in a non-technical, colloquial sense at times.) Basically, and here I follow Jung, I do not permit myself to think in terms of resistances.

So one sees that the attitude of releasing other people into their being-so and from my wishes and demands, of honestly permitting them, on the logical level, to have whatever faults, stupidity, ingratitude, wrong-doings, even perversities and crimes, etc., they may have, applies in this part of the work upon the patient's consciousness too, but now as what the therapist has to practice.

So any *work* on the patient's lack of releasing himself in any one of the discussed senses and areas can only have the form of holding a mirror up to the patient in which he or she can see what they are doing and what this attitude or behavior implies in the way of consequences. "Confronting the patient" here likewise means no more than one's concretely pointing out, exactly describing, and making evident, what needs to be seen; in addition, it could mean expressing how I as therapist feel about it, that, e.g., it pains me to see it, but always in such a way that there is no transgression. My therapeutic reaction has to be laid, as it were, on the table *between* me and the patient, so that as far as I am concerned the patient is free to pick it up from the table or leave it sitting there, and that, in case of his or her having picked it up, he is free to understand and use (process) it the way he or she needs to. That is to say, the patient is also free to misconstrue and misuse it.

2. Working with images, dreams

This work is mainly a craft-like, diligent working with the soul's products. Here the *therapeutēs'* devoted attention to each particular image, his "sticking to the image", with a view to doing justice to it is especially obvious. Despite the fact that this makes up a great part of the work in therapy, it does not need to be treated in this context, since it is the subject of detailed discussions in a whole separate book of mine.[72] The craft-like work on dream images can in turn be in the service of confession, of soul-making and the image process in the narrower sense, as well as in the service of "enlightenment" (which is the topic of the next section). It goes without saying that the work on dreams can also be abused for the purpose of ideology formation and of one's cocooning oneself in a pseudo-subterranean image process.

Where the working with dreams is performed on the basis of a psychology *with* soul, it is particularly essential that the horizon or frame of reference for any interpretation is the objective, autonomous soul as it manifested itself in the whole of cultural history and not the banalities of everyday life and the personal associations of the dreamer. Precisely with respect to the powerful wish of modern people to refer dream images back to the human-all-too-human, to already known conscious contents, and ego desires and fears, the therapist has to be the *vicarius animae* and defend and advocate both the soul standpoint and the dream images as the soul's speaking about itself (and not about people, the dreamers). This is again a different sense of *vicarius animae* from the two earlier ones that we discovered in Chapters III and IV.1, respectively. Here the therapist is this representative of the soul point of view on a conscious level. It is his professional stance.

3. Therapeutic work as "enlightenment" (uncovering and cauterizing hidden illusions, etc.)

An alchemical saying reads: *Omnes superfluitates igne consumuntur*, everything superfluous will be burned away. This saying indicates the spirit of the work to be discussed here.

It is of course a type of therapeutic work that can *not* be applied to *every* case and, within one case, not in *every* single therapeutic situation. It would be completely wrong to come with this kind of approach when a patient just revealed the weakness of the frightened, helpless, wounded person living deep down under the cover of an adult façade. Here this hidden person is an

---

72 I devoted a whole book to this topic: *Working with Dreams. Initiation into the soul's speaking about itself* (forthcoming).

authentic psychological reality that needs to be supported by giving it space to *be*, to show and express itself. Here we are dealing with simple, non-neurotic suffering. Therapy would here probably have to follow the path of one's releasing oneself into the image process as well as Jung's advice to the analyst that the best the analyst can do is not to disturb the process. The coldness of conscious, critical reflection has to be kept away.

By contrast, we might be confronted with a case of a neurotic self-worth problem, with a person's indulging in self-pity, tearful sentimentality and demands on others and on life in general. Here conscious critical reflection is indispensable, the work has to be that of an uncovering of the underlying illusionary assumptions. In general, neurotic conditions are the special sphere of operation for this type of therapeutic work. It takes psychological sensitivity and tact to know which approach fits which therapeutic situation. This type of work takes place in waking consciousness, rather than subterraneously as the seemingly autonomous image process or as effect of the touching of two soul spheres in their totality. The wakefulness of mind and the rational intellect are needed. One has to see through, analytically comprehend, the structure of the neurosis of one's patient. It is a kind of surgical operation. Reduction. The suggestive power[73] of, and participation mystique with, the dominant images, ideals and principles, as well as the patient's secret complicity or fraternization with his neurosis have to be dissolved. One needs the (objective, not subjective) cruelty of a surgeon to do justice to the neurotic patient's own need for disillusionment.

The work necessary here is that of the *objectification of neurosis*. The patient has to be shown exactly where and whenever his or her behavior, reaction, or statement was neurotic, how and in which way precisely, whereby it is necessary to call a spade a spade. E.g., "What you just now said, *this* was your neurosis speaking ..." "With this reaction just now you have fallen into your inferiority (or power or mother or whatever) complex ..." No need to protect the feelings of the patient, because the idea of such a need would surround the neurotic reactions with an aura of awe and taboo, and that would precisely be grist

---

73 Jung: *Suggestivgewalt*, see *GW* 7 § 269.

to the mill of neurosis. But all we are dealing with in neurosis are plain errors, untenable dogmas that one can talk about without much ado, just like mistakes in a pupil's mathematics homework. It simply has to be spelled out where and what the mistake is.

The work on the objectification of neurosis is a kind of craft-like work, too, but not the kind that I said the dream needs, not the *therapeía* of the dream image in the service of soul-making and the anima. It is not one's wholehearted abandon to the images, feelings, inner figures in a spirit of empathy and participation mystique. Archetypal or mythical amplification and the *epistrophê* recommended by James Hillman would by no means be in place here. Rather a critical distance to the phenomena is needed. It is necessary to protect the consciousness of the analyst from falling for the often very cleverly camouflaged neurotic contrivances. What is needed here is a seeing through, not, however, a seeing through to "the God in the phenomenon" as in Hillman's sense, but through the appearance to the logic inherent in the phenomenon, the logical operation that it is the outcome of.

The purpose here is the explicit entrance into psychological adulthood. And the psychological domain in which this type of therapy takes place is that of the animus and not of the anima. Historically speaking we are decidedly in the era of modernity here, modernity with the rupture that lies behind it or gave birth to it, with its duality (the difference between anima and animus). Methodically it is a continuation of the tradition and practice of the Enlightenment.

Above all, this work is one of demythologizing. For as I said, the purpose here is the explicit entrance into psychological adulthood. And we can get a hunch of what this means from a statement by Jung that he made when late in life he was confronted with a letter of his to Freud many decades ago. "For me it [this letter to Freud] is an unfortunately inexpungeable reminder of the incredible folly that filled the days of my youth. The journey from cloud-cuckoo-land back to reality lasted a long time. In my case Pilgrim's Progress consisted in my having to climb down a thousand ladders until I could reach out my hand to the little clod of earth that I am."[74]

---

74 *Letters I*, p. 19, to Freud, 11.II.10, note 8. From letter by Jung of 9.IV.59.

The word demythologizing is not quite accurate. Simply because neurosis has nothing to do with myth and mythology proper anyway, nor with archetypes. Rather, neurosis is the soul's having settled in that kind of cloud-cuckoo-land that consists in abstract principles, absolute dogmas, unconditional claims or demands. Principles are abstract, formal; archetypal images are not. Principles and dogmas are possible only after that fundamental rupture in the history of "the soul" in which consciousness has left the world of myth and entered that of reflection and thought, the world of metaphysics. The absolute principles and unshakeable dogmas constituting neurosis, however, are historically situated in the world of modernity which came after another fundamental historical rupture that severed the soul's bond even with the tradition of metaphysics. Only because of the absoluteness of the principles that are celebrated in neurosis is a *seemingly* "numinous" aura created around the neurotic cloud-cuckoo-land such that it can be confused by the modern mind separated from myth by millennia with the authentic numinosity of the archetypal.

Neurosis in the narrower sense is a kind of deal. "The soul" is willing to accept the person's *empirical* misery, the suffering from all the painful, disturbing, embarrassing symptoms, and to give up the desire for practical happiness, *in exchange for* the *psychological* or *logical* bliss gained through the celebration of its absolute principles and dogmas, principles and dogmas that allow it, "the soul," to dwell in cloud-cuckoo-land high above the *earth*, which in turn on account of this supra-mundane perspective all of a sudden appears as banal and contemptible, just as the life on it appears as simply unthinkable. Therapy has the task of making this deal explicit in all its details, uncovering the particular principles and dogmas at work in this neurosis at hand and subjecting these dogmas to the acid test that will unveil them as untenable, illusionary, and as having been seemingly tenable *only* through the trick of dissociation and cheating (cheating oneself as well as others).

If what the patient has is truly a neurosis in the narrower sense, then this means that it is not the patient who is ill, but only the soul's attitude, ideas, dogmas are sick. Therapy then is in this case not treatment of the person, the human being, the total personality, but work on the ideas, the illusions, and on the deception.[75] An important difference. (Jung, by contrast, still stressed that neurosis was the illness of the whole person.[76]) As therapist I have to credit the patients with basically being healthy and reasonable. I have to impute to them this basic health and first of all relate to *it* (the healthy part) in my therapeutic relation to the patient. I must not let myself be deceived by the initial impressiveness of the neurosis and take it, neurosis, for *real*. I must see through neurosis as something *unreal*, a spook.

The task of therapy here, since it is the work on ideas, has to be mainly intellectual work and has to avoid evoking the will, evoking it, for example, by thinking in terms of resistances. The point is to demonstrate the *errors*, the untenableness of neurosis, not to make the patient fight his neurosis. Because neurosis is in itself and from the outset the fight against itself. Neurosis has to be punctured like a balloon full of hot air. There is nothing to be fought with will-power, nothing to be overcome with effort.[77]

---

75 This distinction between illness of the person and "illness" of the ideas, which is in the case of genuine neuroses a distinction *we* have to make, has become a distinction that the illness itself makes on the phenomenological level in the so-called personality disorders. In such cases, it often happens that the people around the patient suffer more than the patient himself does (or seems to), for example, which they are so vainglorious and impractically idealistic that they become a burden to others.

76 "Its business is not with neuroses but with human beings—that, in fact, is the grand privilege of medical psychology: to treat the whole man and not an artificially segregated function." *CW* 10 § 354. Cf. also *ibid.* §§ 337 and 338. In a way such a view shows the human and spiritual rank of the psychologist Jung. Nevertheless, it is mistaken on several counts. The only thing that factually *can* be treated is the illness, the neurosis. The "whole person" is therapeutically not accessible at all. Secondly, "the whole person" must precisely be *distinguished* from its neurosis as its (or rather the neurotic *soul's*) false thinking. The neurosis must not be projected and loaded upon the person. That would be therapeutically counterproductive. Thirdly, on ethical grounds, the whole person is taboo. We must not focus on it. The whole person of the patient must stay untouched (even theoretically). Fourthly, the idea of "the whole person," alchemy's *homo totus*, belongs on the side of the analyst, not the patient. I can only apply this and similar ideas to the subject, i.e., to *myself*. "The whole person" must not be object, envisioned out there, in the other person, or hoped for as a distant goal of therapy. It is me, the therapist, who has the task to enter into the therapeutic work as *homo totus*. "The whole person" must be the *arché* and spirit of *my* way of conducting therapy.

77 Jung's overcoming his so-called childhood neurosis by sheer willpower and successfully so shows that it was not a full-fledged neurosis stage-managed by the (neurotic) soul alone, but to some extent by the ego-personality. On the

Neurosis does not have a leg to stand on. It is phony through and through. It is the naked emperor—emperor because of its claim of absoluteness and principiality, naked because of the hollowness of this claim. This has to be made evident, nothing more. Or, since this has been evident to the neurotic *soul* itself from the outset (though usually by no means to the ego), "the soul" has to be explicitly confronted with its own implicit knowledge by preventing it from continuing to pull the wool over its own eyes.

The neurotic soul *knows* what it needs to know. But it spitefully does not *want* to draw the necessary consequences from its insight. For example, it knows very well that since my mother has not been giving me the kind of love I would have wished for during these 25 years, it is not to be expected that she will give me this kind of love today or tomorrow. But the neurotic soul insists on counterfactually continuing to expect that. It refuses to release mother, and by analogy all people, into their being "hopeless cases" that will never change, unless a miracle happens; that is, it refuses to release mother from my demand that she be immediately identical with the concept assigned to her (the concept "mother") and to allow her to simply be a human being with her accidental being-so who merely happens to have had the *job* of being my mother.[78]

In general we might say that neurosis is the refusal to enter the real world, that world over whose entrance is, from a psychological point of view, invisibly written the statement from Dante: He who enters here should let go of all hope.[79] This is, of course, not to say that to be in the world would mean to have to be in despair. No, it simply means that one has to let go of the

---

other hand, Jung's "Damn it, one doesn't have fainting fits!" is a clear example of not treating "the whole person", but exclusively only the neurotic mechanism inspired by the neurotic dogma ("I do not have to go to school").

78 Here it is fitting to recall Jung's already cited statement: "a sensible person cannot in all fairness load that enormous burden of meaning, responsibility, duty, heaven and hell, on to the shoulders of one frail and fallible human being—so deserving of love, indulgence, understanding, and forgiveness—who was our mother" (*CW* 9i § 172). "Who was our mother" = who simply happened to have the job of being our mother.

79 Dante, *Divina Commedia*, L'Inferno 3,9: "*Lasciate ogni speranza, voi ch'entrate.*" In Dante, inferno represents a special realm in the other world. But for us it simply reveals for us the deepest essence of earthly, empirical reality.

psychological *mode* of hoping, expecting, of wishful thinking[80] and to attain to an empiricist attitude of waiting and seeing how things and people actually are and in this way allowing oneself to be *taught* by what *is*.[81]

The very point of neurosis, however, is to prevent the natural process of being taught by experience and of drawing consequences from one's insights. The insights are all there, their content is, after all, what the neurotic bemoans and wails about all the time, e.g.: my mother does not love me enough or not in the right way. But the neurotic consciousness does not take the message as an accomplished fact (in the perfect tense), and, above all, does not place itself firmly on this insight as its new ground and standpoint from which to push off to other fields. No, the message is canned: hermetically sealed in a glass vessel or held captive in a gilded cage out there *before* consciousness, in order to preserve it frozen so as to have something that can eternally be stared at in disbelief, disgust, or outrage by consciousness as a mere content or object of consciousness. The insight is taken merely aesthetically and sentimentally, emotionally. With an image we could say, one stares at what is on one's plate and wails about it so as to avoid eating and digesting it, which would have the result that *it* is once and for all *integrated* into one's system (into the form of consciousness) and that one is thus finished with it. It would have been brought to its conclusion. But the very point of neurosis is not to eat what is on one's plate, not to drain one's cup to the dregs.

A drastic and also comical case of this type of neurotic refusal to empty one's cup is the occasionally occurring outcry of patients: "Why do *I* have to go to therapy and work so hard to cure myself? Why do *I* have to waste so much money, time, and effort to recover? After all, it was my parents's maltreatment that caused all my psychic problems. Is it not absolutely unfair that I, who had to suffer so severely from their maltreatment and the ensuing psychological damage done to me, now in addition have

---

80 See above (at the very end of Chapter IV.4) what was said about adulthood and one's having outgrown the future.

81 Here I want to mention again the marvelous quotation from Gotthold Ephraim Lessing. *Was dir ziemt zu tun, ziemt mir, erst zu vernehmen, nicht vorauszusetzen,* With respect to what is your duty to do, it is my duty to hear or learn (if you have done it), not to anticipate and presuppose it. Also, Wilfred Bion's "learning from experience" comes to mind.

to pay the price for the healing of the damage?"

Such patients apply the "polluter-pays principle" valid in the sphere of economics and the environment to the psychological sphere.

It makes no difference whatsoever whether the parents *in fact* maltreated the patient during his childhood and thereby *caused* his psychic problems or whether this accusation against the parents is already part of a neurotic blame-game, a likewise neurotic subterfuge. In either case, the patient's argument would be a neurotic trap. We are here in psychology, not in the economic or social sphere. The "polluter-pays principle" does not apply. What or who the *cause* of the wounds was is totally irrelevant. If I broke a leg because of my own carelessness, or if my leg was broken because someone else pushed me down the stairs, it is and remains *my* pain and *my* having to wear a cast on my leg and *my* being unable to walk freely for a while. The damage is MINE, and if I WANT to overcome it, it is of course I who has to do something about it. It does not help me a bit if the person who threw me down the stairs gets punished.

My answer to such a patient's complaint about the alleged unfairness might, for example, be something like this: "But you don't *have to* exert your own effort to cure yourself. You don't *have to* come to therapy. You can also stay at home and do nothing about your problems and wounds. Nobody forces you. The only question is: What do YOU prefer? Do YOU *want to* be cured—or do you not? If you are satisfied with *not* being cured, you don't need to do anything. However, if YOU wish to be cured, then of course YOU have to pay the price of exerting your energy. It is entirely up to you. It's YOUR choice. Nobody else cares whether you are healthy or not. But maybe YOU care?" Jung wrote in similar spirit, "But no matter how much parents and grandparents may have sinned against the child, the man who is really adult will accept these sins *as his own condition* which has to be reckoned with. Only a fool is interested in other people's guilt, since he cannot alter it. The wise man learns only from his own guilt" (*CW* 12 § 152, my emphasis).

Psychologically this complaint at work in the patient's thinking shows that he has no *motivation* for therapy. He is like a baby that thinks when it is hungry, someone else, the *mother*, has to immediately come and feed it. For a baby, this is appropriate. Not for a grown-up patient.

Motivation for therapy means: the patient understands that *his* illness is *only his* problem and *his* responsibility, that he does not so much *have* a problem but *is* the problem. From the realization that this is so it follows that HE—his thinking, his attitude, his form of consciousness—needs to change.

Trying to put in the described way the blame and responsibility on others, the parents, for example, is a naive, childish form of defense. It operates on the external-reality or social level, the level of people and their interactions. A much more subtle and tricky defense stays internal and works with a logical shift, the move away from cognition and sober analysis to sentiments and emotions. We could call it the *defense mechanism of emotionalization*. The sober knowledge of an experienced bad event is translated into a personal emotion. It is not only a frequent defense on the part of patients, but is very often also supported by therapists, often even "institutionalized" in the very form of particular therapies, namely, in those forms of therapy that put feelings in the center. Together patient and therapist then revel in the emotions of how painful, how unendurable events in the patient's life were, how terrible the loss of parents through death or divorce was, how helpless the child was, and the adult patient still is, on account of all that happened to him. *Trauerarbeit*, (work of) grieving, is thought to be necessary (this *concept* is in itself neurotic). A lot of crying over spilt milk.

As indicated, very often all this is a (typically and exclusively modern[82]) neurotic defense against the *simple cognition of the truth*, against the acceptance of the facts of the patient's biography, against letting them *be*. Instead of seeing that something *is* (objectively) terribly sad, grieving work wants (subjectively) to do a lot of *crying* over spilt milk. With it one prefers to make a fuss about it and indulge in the misery. It is really not very interesting nor important whether something was a bad event or not. What is, however, psychologically important is *that* it is or was exactly what and how it was. The adult "will accept these sins [of parents or grandparents against the child, but we could also add: all these painful fates] *as his own*

---

82 This is of course pleonastic, inasmuch as neurosis as such (in the strict sense) is intrinsically a *modern* phenomenon.

condition", we have just heard Jung say, and Hegel had more than a century earlier made the essential point that

> Greek man, having the mindset of necessity, calms down by saying to himself: It is so, nothing can be done about it; I must put up with it. ... By standing on this standpoint and saying: that's the way it is, he has put aside every particularity, has renounced and abstracted from all special purposes, interests. ... There is ... no consolation for man available [but also not needed]. Consolation is needed (only) in so far as he demands compensation for the loss; but here he needs no compensation, he has given up the inner root of what he has lost. What he has given up, he has completely given up.[83]

What the man who is really adult and who is freed from his neurosis has acquired, even if he is not an ancient Greek, is this *mindset of necessity*. Psychotherapy has to aim for an attitude for which the inner root of what has been lost has been given up, has been written off completely. Grieving in the sense of *Trauerarbeit* is the (neurotic) decision spitefully and counterfactually within oneself to *hold on to* what is already *known* to have been lost and the refusal to give it up root and branch. The harping on feelings and emotions is psychotherapy's neurotic program of infantilization and dwelling in the ego. We may recall here also Jung's essential dictum, "If you are adapted you need no emotion. ... it is simply a lack of adaptation, that you are not up to the situation. ... So to have an emotion is to be on the way to a morbid condition ..."[84] What Jung referred to with "lack of adaptation" and with not being "up to the situation" is precisely (in our context of a loss) the soul's not having wholeheartedly *given up* and *written off* what is known to have been lost.

Another favorite question with which neurosis is defended is: "why is my mind dominated by these neurotic principles, what made it so?" The simple answer to this question is: because *I* (or rather the soul in me) love these principles; *I* want them, believe to need them, consider them absolutely indispensable. They have no cause other than *my* own clinging to them and defending them

---

83 G.W.F. Hegel, *Vorlesungen über die Philosophie der Religion*, Teil 2: "Die bestimmte Religion", newly edited by Walter Jaeschke, Hamburg (Meiner: Philos. Bibl. vol. 460) 1994, pp. 381f. and 543f. My transl. (The text in square brackets appears in a footnote to line 877 and represents a variant from another transcript of this Hegel lecture.)
84 C.G. Jung, *Nietzsche's* Zarathustra. *Notes of the Seminar Given in 1934-1939*, ed. by James L. Jarrett, Princeton (Bollingen Series XCIX, Princeton Univ. Pr.) 1988, vol. 2, pp. 1497 f.

as my dearest treasure, a treasure maybe even dearer to me than my life, but at least dearer than my practical well-being.

In this context it is unavoidable to at least mention the usual illusion occurring in the neurotic that he or she wants to overcome their neurosis. It is true, neurotics *wish* to be free of it or at least of the unpleasant effects of it, but they don't *want* to be free of it. A crucial difference. *Empirically* they would honestly like to be free of it, while *psychologically* they would not dream of giving it up. Wishing happens in cloud-cuckoo-land, it's like daydreaming. It does not cost anything to wish for something. To *will* something is an entirely different matter. It means the readiness to do whatever it takes to realize it. The typically neurotic dissociation of an idle empirical wish and a diametrically opposed psychological *real* insistence has to be exposed. The patient has to understand that his empirical wish to be freed of the neurosis is pure theory. It can be forgotten. It does not count. It is a thousand times offset by the psychological insistence.

I said a while ago that the neurotic soul knows what it needs to know and began with the example of one's mother as a hopeless case. Other frequent fundamental insights that the neurotic soul already has, but spitefully refuses to let become its own real standpoint from which to live life, are the following:

1. I am psychologically, metaphysically all alone in the world ("*mutterseelenallein*"). Jung spoke of the "illimitable loneliness of man" (*Letters 2*, p. 586, to Berann, 27.VIII.60). I am—psychologically—all alone "in the dead emptiness of interstellar space," "where, in the cold light of consciousness, the blank barrenness of the world reaches to the very stars" (*CW* 9i § 31+29). Even if empirically there is somebody who loves me and really means *me*, metaphysically I am not meant, in the sense that Christ was meant at the event of his baptism, where a voice from heaven said: "Thou art my beloved son; in thee I am well pleased." I am all on my own; an atomic subjectivity. I am merely a little clod of earth. *Ultimately*, i.e., metaphysically, nobody cares two hoots about me, about whether I exist or not and if I feel well or miserable. Only I care.

2. The world, life as a whole, is not a priori contained in a sacral aura, in a higher meaning, in something absolute that would elevate existence from the merely pragmatic empirical level; there is no master plan for life, no divine order in which

everything and every event has its ordained place. No, what happens is contingent. And so I am exposed to the vicissitudes of life. Even in a modern city, life is life in the jungle where one has to watch out for oneself and might get through pretty well or not so well or not get through at all.

3. My fellow human beings are not walking ideals, not identical with the *concepts* of their *offices* or jobs ("mother," "father," "doctor," "judge," "teacher," "spouse", etc.). They, too, are as a matter of course merely little clods of earth and fallible, just human, all-too-human. I have to release them from my expectation that they are a priori identical with their concepts.

4. There is no solid ground that would support me. *I* have to *be* my own ground, *exist* as my own ground or perish.

5. I am nobody special. I am just one of millions or billions of people.

6. Nothing is a priori provided for me. "Oh, I see, here in life one has the work!" (Jung's insight that ended his childhood neurosis). I have to become active myself, make my own bed, and as I made it, so I have to lie in it. True, there is no moral obligation to make my bed, but if I did not make it, then I will not have a bed to lie in. I have to be my own mother and father. Even if my literal parents are alive and are good to me—inasmuch as I am an adult, I have no parents, I am not their child anymore. They and I are on the same level, that of adulthood, sort of colleagues. If I want to get good at something, I have to learn and practice. If I want a relationship, I have to go and find someone and slowly establish a relationship. Everything takes time. One step has to be taken after the other.

7. Life is nothing other than draining my cup to the dregs, fulfilling my lot. I have to eat what life has put on my plate without looking to the left or right and comparing if others have something better on their plate. It does not matter what *they* have got. The only thing for me is *my* plate and what is on *it*. I only have this life of mine. *This* is it! There is no alternative, no choice. In life I am not still *before* the meal, as if in a restaurant where I am offered a menu; no, the meal has already been going on for some time, I find myself in the middle of it; the point of "ordering" is long past, and *I* never had any say in it. In life I am not in a supermarket with thousands of options. Life is not optional. It is factual, determined. Even as it is still going on, it

always takes place in the form of the perfect tense, as what *has* happened and what thus is an accomplished fact. The point is to always catch up with the prefect tense, to reach the goal set for me with each factual event, to finish what has been served to me in each case as *my* cup of sorrows or of delight, *but not* to waste any time on thinking about whether my dish is good or not and what else I might possibly have gotten on it. I have to start to eat and finish my plate.

8. If I have been wronged or wounded, nobody else but I myself have to pay the price, as I pointed out earlier. *Empirically-practically* I may perhaps get damages, but *psychologically* it is I who has to balance out the wrong with *psychological gold*: with the honest suffering of the pain that it caused me, and that not only passively with the feeling of being a *victim*, but by actively appropriating the harm I experienced, making it truly my own, so that it is no longer an external *fact* that *befell* me, but the inner truth of this fact that is appropriated as my own insight, my knowledge.

9. Life is dangerous. Living in the world, we are potentially exposed to illnesses, crimes, terror attacks, the cruelty of dictators, injustice, the falsehood, ill-will, or nastiness of other people, and so on. Existence in the real world inevitably includes to get marred, wounded. Wounds and misery are a normal part or possibility of life on earth.[85] I cannot live and expect to go through

---

85 This needs to be kept in mind in view of the reaction sometimes to be observed in psychological, especially Jungian, circles to such events as the terror attacks on September 11, 2001 or the present corona virus pandemic. The one reaction I have in mind is the blowing up of such events to "traumas" and the psychologists's need to fantasize that these "traumas" would as a matter of course lead to psychic conditions of anxiety or might even bring about a malignant regression, for which reason such psychologists preemptively offer their services (just as after serious train or airplane accidents with many wounded and dead, psychologists are routinely and preemptively sent to the place of accident because one *wants* people to feel and *makes* them feel "traumatized" and helpless to live through such events of life on their own—really sick!). No doubt, some people in the modern West are only waiting for appropriate opportunities to react hysterically. But it is terrible if psychologists don't see through these hysterics but take them absolutely seriously as effects naturally caused by these "traumatic" events. They then ride the same hobby-horse as the patient. Jung once raised the question: "is it an object worthy of anxiety, or a poltroonery, i.e., the I's shitting its pants?" (*Letters 1*, p. 333, to Künzli, 16 March 1943, transl. modif.), having in mind as a *worthy* object something like "the almighty shadow of the Lord, which is the

3. Therapeutic work as "enlightenment"

life untouched, immaculate, in-nocent. Ultimately life even means to *be heading for* death.

All this is known and understood by the neurotic soul. But it is *declared* to be absolutely unacceptable, even unthinkable. This is the neurotic contradiction (and what makes it neurotic).

Or it is at least *one* of the contradictions as which neurosis exists. Another one we have encountered already a number of times: that neurosis *is* the defense or fight against *itself*. Neurosis exists because it makes the neurotic want to get rid of it. Now we come to a third, the opposite contradiction (with which I refer back to my earlier assertion that in neurosis it is not the *person* who is ill). The neurotic in this case tries to get rid of his neurosis by swallowing it, by declaring himself ill, deficient, psycho-logically handicapped. He identifies with it. This has to be seen through as a defense of the neurosis, as hiding behind one's neurosis in order to protect *it* from being detected and X-rayed. The neurotic has to learn to comprehend that he has *everything he needs within* himself. At bottom, there is nothing wrong with him. He is just a normal human being. With all his weaknesses he is perfect. What *is* wrong, sick, neurotic, is the *thinking*, the dogmas, principles, expectations, demands at work in him, *not* he.

This is also why *the patient* does not have to change. He does not have to *do* anything, does not need to *change* anything. On the contrary, he as active and willing subject has to step back and stay out of it. *It*, his secret thinking, has to change. And that cannot *be* changed at will, by dictate. It has to change, and that

---

fear that fills heaven and earth". See also above at the very end of Chapter IV.4 what was said about worries concerning the future. People in countries like Afghanistan or Iraq live with and actually experience the most brutal terror attacks on an almost daily basis with numerous people being torn to pieces by explosives. But no hysterics, no anxiety condition, and no psychologists, just a sober, rational, very realistic *fear*. It seems to me that since the end of World War II people in the West have lived enwrapped in an illusionary bubble of peace, safety, and wealth—an absolute exception and luxury. The corona virus crisis has at least for the moment shattered this bubble a little and perhaps brings us momentarily back a tiny bit down to earth and in contact with real reality: life as life in a "jungle" with real dangers. The second reaction of some Jungian psychologist I have encountered is to want to see the corona virus pandemic as sent by the soul and as expressive of an archetype. A clear mystification. Superstition. This pandemic is a plain natural occurrence. The soul has nothing to do with it and no interest in it.

means *dissolve*, of its own accord. But in order for it to be able to change, all that is needed is that he *enters*, with both his critical consciousness and with his heart, the secret chamber of his thoughts and makes himself present there, settles there. This he has to do indeed. It is somewhat like with the descent into the underworld where one had to give the shades of the dead blood to drink to enable them to speak a bit. He has to give some of the blood of his conscious mind to the ghostly hidden principles operative in his neurosis and thus end their dissociation from consciousness. Once they are unreservedly in consciousness, they cannot hold up. However, to get to a point where they are truly unreservedly in consciousness, where consciousness fully owns them, is rather difficult and probably rare. More often, consciousness merely "peeps" at them from the safe distance of the ego or the intellect. In this way it only becomes aware of the semantic content of the highest principles that are the soul of the person's neurosis and can think *about* them and their stupidity, but it cannot *think* them. This is a crucial difference.

Similarly in the case of a dream with a so-called "negative" image or "negative" ending it would be totally wrong to want anything changed, to be better, more "positive." This would be an ego manipulation. Let us take as an example the following dream image: "I am supposed to move into a house. It is dilapidated, terribly neglected." The ego reaction might be the moral imperative to end the neglect, to get the house back in order. But psychologically this would be entirely the wrong move. And it would be the refusal to do what the dream tells me to do. The dream wants me to move into the *dilapidated* house, not to move into the house that I, at least in my moralistic thoughts, have already fixed up into a nice cozy home. In the direction that my thoughts take, I have already ridded myself of the house into which I am supposed to move, replaced it by a better one. But we have to stick to the image. The move into this house means to settle in and occupy precisely the dilapidation, the neglect, the error, the wrong, the wound. I have to enter the dilapidated house *with my heart*, my feeling, as well as my *critical consciousness*. No more, and nothing else. The dilapidation does not need to be corrected, to be eliminated by me as ego, through my behavior (and be it only an imaginal, rather than a literal behavior). No, if there is to be a change for the better, it has to be the dilapidation's own, autonomous change.

Paradoxically, the psychological truth is that by (mentally, imaginally) cleaning the house up and thus getting rid of the neglect, the *neglect* itself in "the soul" remains unaltered. It has only been pushed in some other dark corner. And the dilapidation can only change the way *it* may want to change, if it has been nourished with my blood, my soul, my wholehearted presence, has been attached to the conscious life of the *homo totus*, the whole personality. It needs to be owned, unreservedly felt in its dilapidatedness. That is all it needs, but it is obviously what we are least willing to give. We prefer to fob the dream off with some similar looking substitute that, however, through our wish to improve it, is totally different, indeed diametrically opposed. Apparently, rather than *receiving* the possible change *from* the dilapidation as *its* self-movement, *its* own transformation from within itself, we insist on being in control of any change, if change has become unavoidable.

Much the same has to be said about the not infrequent dreams about a neglected starving child, for example, that the dreamer finds in the cellar of his or her house. The point here is not to correct this situation by literally feeding the child and ending its starvation. No, quite the contrary, it is the neglect and the *starving* of the child which should *psychologically* or *logically* be fed with the dreamer's heart, mind and soul.

In the course of a longer psychotherapy of a neurotic condition, one by one the secret dogmas have to be pulled out of their hiding and brought into the limelight. The patient has to lend them *his* voice. The dogmas should not be fought, condemned, overcome. There should not be a police or prosecutor attitude towards them. No prohibition, no blame, no "should not," "ought not to be," no moralizing. Also no disparagement. Not the hermeneutic of suspicion in the spirit of wishing to tear masks from a person's face. One should conversely *welcome* the complexes and dogmas on the stage of consciousness and open-mindedly listen to them. They should be given a fair chance. They should be allowed, and even urged, to state their case. But then it will become apparent that they have no case. The emperor is indeed naked. And so the dogmas will crumble away, falling to dust like ancient mummies exposed to the air, no will-power and effort to overcome them being needed.

The problem of a complex or neurotic principle is that its status is such that it is much like the witch in a fairytale from 1001 Nights. A young man is walking on a road through the desert and sees a poor, weak old woman sitting helplessly at the side of the road. He has pity on her and carries her on his back. As he continues his way, she is getting heavier and heavier and drives him on from behind.—*This* is the complex. One has shouldered it "out of pity" or some other *feeling*. It then sits in one's back and as such is invisible, intangible, it only makes itself felt through its weight, that is to say, it has mainly the character of an atmosphere. An atmosphere is all around one, envelops one from all sides. By letting the complex come forward and having it show itself, it is turned into a *limited* and *concrete* object of, and *before*, consciousness so that now it can be looked at and named, described; one can have a distance to it and thus *examine* it with respect to its legitimacy. Its atmosphere character, its magic aura, and ipso facto its unquestionable power is gone. Another fairytale comes to mind here: Rumpelstiltskin. The goblin of this name was powerful as long as its name was unknown. But the moment it was called by its name, it had to tear itself apart.

So far so good. But this pulling the dogmas and complexes into the light of day and letting them state their case has to be repeated many times. The end of a neurosis is not a one-time event of one single insight. It is true that each time the dogma has in this way been openly welcomed, it indeed crumbles away. But each dogma or complex is like a book that exists in thousands of copies. What crumbled away was merely one single copy of it. With another image that I have from a one-time analyst teacher of mine, Hildegard Buder, we could say that each time that a neurotic dogma has been truly seen through is like having cut a single thread of a thick rope. But many threads make up one strand, and several strands make up the rope. The rope will tear only once maybe three quarters of the threads will have been cut. So a long time of "working through" will be necessary, a working through not only in the analytical session and with the help of the analyst, but also and mainly by the patient himself outside the consulting room in all sorts of daily-life situations.

VI. The therapeutic effect through newness and through movement as such

Every *new* theory or technique has a special therapeutic potential that is greater than that of well-established theories or techniques, and for this reason the greater therapeutic effect also wears down in the course of time, as this new theory or technique is becoming established. It has also been said occasionally that especially difficult or hopeless looking cases should be given into therapy to a beginner, because such a beginner is not yet burdened down with negative experiences and goes to work freshly and with undiminished enthusiasm. I do not know whether this is really a good idea, but at any rate it is an indication for the view that what here is seen as the true therapeutic factor is the freshness of the attitude and the zest themselves, the enthusiasm, the beginner's vivacious application to the work, rather than what one has learned, the theory that one adheres to or a therapist's long practical experience.

In neurosis and some other psychic disorders, the logical life of "the soul" has been arrested. The soul is stuck, circles around in the same groove. *One* Now that is already past nevertheless rules over the present and all future. This is the background. Therapy aims at getting what is stuck into movement again and to make fluid what has solidified and become hardened. We see against this backdrop why newness has a vivifying effect. It is refreshing, surprising. Thus the point here is not whether the new approach is a much better one than previous ones, in itself more convincing, a deeper theory or technique, or "the true answer" to the psychological problem in comparison to other approaches; the question is not whether it has scientific merit and dignity or is not perhaps rather a quack approach. What I am trying to suggest is much rather that it is the naked character and degree of newness as such that gives a new theory or technique its therapeutic benefit. It is the fact that the wind of spirit that bloweth here makes itself felt.

It is not only the newness of a new theory or method that has this special therapeutic effect. Also the initial phase of any therapy may at times produce greater effects in a shorter time than one can expect later on in the same therapy. In the initial phase, everything is new for the patient, and this newness lifts his soul a bit off the ground. When then, after some months or even years, therapy has become a routine, every Wednesday afternoon, any therapeutic effect has to be gained through much more work. And often the changes reached through the initial effect do also not *last*. Obviously, in such a case "the soul" has come down again to the ground from its at first having been uplifted, without having been able to bring anything back with it from up there, its short-term elated state.

Very often therapists who come up with a new therapeutic theory or method are completely captivated by it and enthused by it, filled with it. They totally believe in it, without much or any critical distance. This may be one aspect of the strong effect on patients. The strong belief and enthusiasm have something inspiring, charismatic and thus even seductive and contagious. In such a case and in this sense, the new theory makes unconscious, cocooning consciousness in the new theory, creating a new believer and adherent. Practically, from the ego point of view, this may be beneficial as far as the patient's symptoms are concerned, but, psychologically seen, the unconsciousness and the believer-status are of course a totally undesirable effect.

But there is possibly also an opposite aspect. To the extent that the newness of the theory opens something up, breaks something open that had been stuck, it may also have an effect of making conscious. Although it may have this effect perhaps only implicitly, *ansichseiend*, we may nevertheless also have to consider the possibility of a genuine, explicit (*fürsichseiend*) increase of conscious awareness. Here once more comes above all to mind Freud's statement about the "*Junktim von Heilen und Forschen*" , the inseparable oneness of healing effect and research spirit. Freud states that it was the insight (i.e., the analyst's insight) that brought the therapeutic success; one could not treat patients without learning something new, and one did not gain any insight (or enlightenment, illumination) without experiencing its beneficial effect.[86] A wonderful statement. What Freud at least

---

86 See Sigmund Freud, *The Question Of Lay Analysis*, Translated from the German and Edited by James Strachey. Garden City, New York (Anchor Books, Doubleday & Company) 1964, p. 109.

implicitly indicates is that it was not so much the factual correctness of the insight that produced the effect, but the *event* of the emergence of an insight, its inspiring quality, the fact that it gave wings to the spirit. Therapy as a true *intellectual adventure*, as exploration in a new continent, not as the application of an already known theory. Curiosity, research as *process* and *performance*, not as the bureaucratic attempt of adding new building bricks to the cathedral of psychological knowledge, not as new contributions to a *doctrine*. The view here expressed by Freud ties in with Jung's statement discussed earlier that the patient must be of personal interest to the therapist on account of the material that he brings to the analyst, or on account of the substance of the human problem he represents.

Newness is here simply the *positive* form of movement and fluidity. *They* are the actual therapeutic factors, not the literal newness as such. A new theory inspires the patient because the therapist is inspired, and the therapist can be inspired because the theory is still in the state of becoming and thus of movement. It has not congealed to the form of a doctrine yet. It is still in flux, still in the status of logical negativity, still not positivized.

But it is the fate of everything new to turn into something customary. What once was process and exploration takes on the form of a fixed doctrine or even of an ideology or a routinely applied technique. Thus what initially had the effect of opening things up and opening doors of awareness, has turned around and now fixates and cocoons consciousness, makes *consciousness* unconscious. The time of orthodoxy has come. Now all the former living insights have become fully positivized, components of a static theory or technical instruments to be applied to what then is no more than "a case."

This brings to mind a quotation from Jung in response to hearing about debates about certain Jungian concepts by some of his followers, debates in which according to him "many words (had been) buzzing about": "From such discussions we see what awaits me once I have become posthumous. Then everything that was once fire and wind will be bottled in spirit and reduced to dead nostrums. Thus are the gods interred in gold and marble and ordinary mortals like me in paper" (*Letters 2*, p. 469, to von der Heydt, 22 December 1958). It is the movement from *fire and wind* to dead words on paper.

131

The reason for this change[87] is the dialectic of the soul's logical life, which is the movement from de-objectifying to objectifying and back (*Entgegenständlichung* and *Vergegenständlichung*), from reification to logification, from projection and acting out to interiorization[88] or integration, from logical life (as performative and process) to ontologized theory, alchemically speaking from *solutio* to *coagulatio* and back. Everything, as, for example, both Hegel and the Chinese I Ching knew, moves into its opposite. A living insight or a living tradition moves by itself into its own death as a rigid, solidified positivity, *unless* it is renewed time and again through reformations or revolutions that push off from the sterile form into which the tradition has sunk. It is the fairytale motif of the old king and the dragon guarding the way to the water of life. The dragon demands that every so often young life has to be sacrificed to it, and it takes the hero of the fairytale to free the country of the dragon and renew the kinghood.

This dialectic is rooted in our linguistic nature. Wilhelm von Humboldt expressed the dialectic of language in the following way:

> Through the same act by virtue of which man exudes language out of himself, he cocoons himself in it, and each language draws around the nation to which it belongs a circle; this circle can be left only insofar as one at the same time enters the circle of another language.[89]

Applied to our specific topic we can say that the very act through which the refreshing newness of a new insight or theory comes into the world begins to establish the cocoon in which consciousness will slowly have settled and become lifeless, a repeated

---

87 Leaving aside the other obvious, but *external* reason of the difference between the originator of a body of thought, *in* whom all the concepts are alive and dissolved in the living whole of his thought) and his disciples who merely try to take its elements over as ready-mades.

88 I do not use the term "introjection," which was used by Jung, because the content is not "thrown" inside (a *spatial* movement), but rather decomposed, evaporated, sublimated: deepened into its own notion. One has to remember here that interiorization translates *Erinnerung*, the other, ordinary-language meaning of which is remembering, recollection.

89 "*Durch denselben Act, vermöge welches der Mensch die Sprache aus sich heraus spinnt, spinnt er sich in dieselbe ein, und jede Sprache zieht um die Nation, welcher sie angehört, einen Kreis, aus dem es nur insofern hinauszugehen möglich ist, als man zugleich in den Kreis einer andren Sprache hinübertritt.*"

routine. Maybe this is the same as the fact that birth, the beginning of life, *is* the slow but certain *heading for* death.

Although this movement from newness to sterile routine may be inevitable, therapeutic psychology must do its best to prevent itself from coagulating into something fixed, because it cannot be genuinely therapeutic if it has been substantiated into a theory or a technique to be applied. Psychology, although it will time and again find itself in the status of a doctrine, must not *be* in the form of a doctrine. Even with respect to its intellectual and theoretical aspects, psychology must be *performative*, a *practice*, a *method*. It must be "fire and wind". Its theorizing must be released into the Now and to be acquired from within each now afresh. Here I want to refer back to what I said earlier about improvisation.

Intersubjectivity and universal validity and ahistorical generality are unpsychological. Psychology cannot have the form of a science in the conventional sense of this word. Jung charged Freud, this was one of the main criticisms he raised against him, that he had turned his method into a theory. In other words, Jung accused Freud of having "ontologized", Hillman might have said: literalized, what should have stayed performative, a way of doing. I believe, however, that Jung unwittingly did much the same, of course in other regards and ways. In *Memories, Dreams, Reflections*, he uses, to describe the origin and development of his life's work an image that expresses this positivizing quite unmistakingly. He speaks of his having first been confronted with hot, liquid magma, which then cooled down and hardened into stone, a stone that thereafter could be hewn by him.

Against Freudian psychoanalysis Jung once raised the charge, part of which was already quoted in another context above:

> Psychoanalysis is evidently a technique behind which the human being vanishes, and which always remains the same no matter whether X, Y, or Z practices it. Consequently, the psychoanalyst needs no self-knowledge and no criticism of his presuppositions. Apparently the purpose of his training analysis is to make him not a human being but a correct applier of technique (*CW* 10 § 350, transl. modif.).

We need not examine here to what extent this criticism is justly raised against psychoanalysis or not. It is more important to extract the general principle, here applied to psychoanalysis, and apply it each to oneself and beyond oneself perhaps also generally to the training of Jungian analysts practiced nowadays at the various training institutes and to the role of the *International Association of Analytical Psychology* in disseminating Jungian thought all over the world. Where are the theoretical presuppositions of analysts in training really examined? At which institute is a serious and living critical reflection of psychological theory going on in the first place so that the personal reflection of the unspoken theoretical presuppositions of training candidates could have a chance in their training analyses? Where is Jungian theory not taught as a fixed *doctrine*, as theoretically wishy-washy and often syncretistically mixed with other theoretical elements?

The dialectic that Humboldt pointed out is inescapable. How then can psychology/psychotherapy avoid becoming a positivity, a substantiated theory? In order to understand this we have to realize that this dialectic refers only to any language as a whole, not to the individual utterance. The individual utterance belongs to the Now and will only last as long as this Now extends into the future. It will of its own accord gradually sink into oblivion, unless of course it is artificially held on to, petrified. We can take this as a hint for psychology, too. Should it not be possible to stay in the Now, to refuse to establish a substantiated theory, to ontologize what is actually a doing, a performance, or to turn into a doctrine what is actually the *event* of an insight—without, however, becoming untheoretical[90]? To stay in the Now, of course, not in the sense of eternalizing this one now, but precisely by letting the one now go by when its time has come and allowing it to change into a different now, so that staying in the Now would mean going along with the eachness of moments within the flow of time. In other words, should it not be possible to live with respect to one's psychological theorizing *from hand to mouth*?

---

90 "Paracelsus ... emphasized that nobody could be a doctor who did not understand the art of 'theorizing' [*die Kunst des 'Theoricierens'*]" (*CW* 16 § 218), Jung on his part emphasized, and a few lines later spoke of, the "*Heilkraft der Auffassung*", the healing power of the theoretical conception, or, as he said elsewhere, the *theoria* (which is not to be confused with our modern sense of theory). (The *Collected Works* translate "Heilkraft der Auffassung" in a wishy-washy common-sense way as "healing power of a man's mental attitude", as so often with no insight into what Jung was actually talking about. As if "a man's mental attitude" required a special art! Everybody has a mental attitude.)

Jung's image was that of hot liquid magma. It is in the nature of magma to slowly cool down and turn into hard rock. But we could just as well start out from his other image of fire, a flame, where the natural consequence would not be a positive result, but the dying down of the flame precisely when the combustible material in its positivity has been totally consumed by it. The flame consumes what is positive and feeds off it. It is the image of the move from positivity to logical negativity. And the flame is committed to negativity by rather dying than, for the purpose being able to keep itself in existence, having to pay the price of becoming positivized.

Or, instead of fire and flame we could also think of water. An alchemical saying states that one should not begin any operation until everything has become water, i.e., fluid, has reached the logical status of fluidity.

Our thinking of the individuation process has been fundamentally informed by two images or conceptions. The one is from mythology, the other from alchemy. I am thinking of Dionysian dismemberment, on the one hand, and of the process of fermenting corruption, solution, sublimation, distillation, evaporation, on the other. Both describe the movement back from stone into magma, from positivity to logical negativity, from coagulation to fluidity or pneuma, spirit. Such a process means for the *person* the experience of the dissolution of the conception of his or her personality *as* a substance or substrate, as an ontological entity, a positivity. Now, if therapy wants to enable those who go into therapy to experience this movement, does not the logic or concept of *therapy itself* have to have undergone this movement in the first place? And does it not have to hold itself in this movement, as the horizon, the fiery spirit, and the logic of the whole Work?

What else could this mean but that our theorizing has (by no means been abolished but) been delivered over to the Now and thus to the negativity of "the soul's" logical life?

The fountain of life and similar symbols, rather than being the one great mysterious, hard to attain *goal* of a grand quest, may well be right here; and to drink from this fountain may be no more than the simple continuous release (*Einkehr*) of the logic of our being and theorizing into the Now. Theorizing not as ontologizing but performative. Theoretical concepts not projected

135

into the distance and future as goals to be attained, but as a reality of the ongoing present, informing our own thinking. And not mystified as belonging into the otherworldly realm of archetypes, but as the inner truth of each moment. No more than *Augenblicks"götter"*, momentary "gods".[91] Fulfilled moments.

---

91 The term comes from Hermann Usener's book, *Götternamen* (1896).

VII. Limits

Often psychotherapists seem to be buoyed up by the deep-seated, implicit or even explicit, belief that through the therapy it should theoretically, in principle, be possible for all psychic problems to be resolved, that through psychotherapy and enough therapeutic effort it should be possible to relieve all people from their psychological symptoms and disorders. One only needs to analyze neuroses long and carefully enough and they will be removed.[92] Understanding the neurotic mechanisms is all that is needed. Difficulties and conflicts between people, especially lovers or partners, only require that these people learn how to talk about their problems with each other appropriately; then their relationship will be fine. All psychic problems are merely the result of misunderstandings or false reaction to, false processing of "traumatic" experiences. What went wrong during the first years of life in a patient's development, can be healed through the appropriate psychotherapeutic treatment.

It could be that it is inherent in the logic of the institution of such a thing as "psychotherapy" itself to entertain such ideas in psychotherapists, although their own experience with the analysts and teachers at their own training institutes, all of whom have as a matter of course undergone years of analysis and sometimes an "individuation process" in Jung's sense, could already have cured them of these optimistic beliefs in the power of analysis and psychotherapy. For, as Adolf Guggenbühl-Craig in his cited article on "What works in psychotherapy?"[93] rightly pointed out

> Many excellent therapists are themselves seriously neurotic; most therapists have great trouble in social contact, etc. Thus there is often

---

92 Sometimes this belief of psychotherapists goes even much further, to the idea that through the therapy of a large proportion of the whole population the world could become a better world; politicians should be analyzed; psychology should be applied to politics, etc. A crazy illusion. The title of James Hillman's book (together with Michael Ventura, San Francisco [HarperSanFranisco] 1992) already expressed the realization that the opposite is true: "We've had a hundred years of psychotherapy and the world's getting worse".

93 See footnote 4.

> hardly a trace of the healer [archetype] having been constellated in him
> or in her personally. The same can be said with respect to the
> individuation of psychotherapists. They are often not more individuated
> than their analysands (*op. cit.*, p. 34, my transl.).

And of course, *consciously* therapists are fully aware of the
limited success of their work, of the uncertain prognosis in many
cases, and do not expect too much. But underneath this practical
realism the described optimistic illusion seems to be alive
undisturbed by experience and to be what ultimately sustains
and drives the therapeutic impulse.

But maybe it is the other way around. It is not the institution
and logic of psychotherapy that seduces its adherents into
entertaining such beliefs and hopes, but it is much rather that
those persons who choose, for example, Jungian psychotherapy as
their future profession are from the outset motivated by the deep-
seated wish to cure and help and they, as persons, bring it and
their wishful thinking into the objective profession. What is
seductive would in this case be the persons' own desires. It is
their inner need to believe that all could be well; that one just
needs to talk long enough about the issues (psychotherapy as
"talking cure"!) and try to understand dreams correctly (in which
the curing impulses are imagined to be presented as if on a silver
platter to consciousness), and healing will happen.

Where psychotherapy is inspired or even driven by such deep
personal desires and psychic needs, the mentioned fantasies and
hopes are to be understood as being merely the congealed
objectified form of these needs. Psychotherapy is then in the grip
of the ego. Here the reminiscence of Freud's personal admission
may have a healthy sobering impact:

> After forty-one years of medical activity, my self-knowledge tells me that
> I have never really been a doctor in the proper sense. I became a doctor
> through being compelled to deviate from my original purpose; and the
> triumph of my life lies in my having, after a long and roundabout
> journey, found my way back to my earliest path. I have no knowledge of
> having had any craving in my early childhood to help suffering
> humanity.[94]

Jung likewise admitted that the dominant force in himself was
the "daimon of creativity" (*MDR* p. 358) and that "Many excited

---

94 Sigmund Freud, *The Question Of Lay Analysis*, Translated from the German
    and Edited by James Strachey. Garden City, New York (Anchor Books,
    Doubleday & Company) 1964, pp 104 f.

in me a feeling of living humanity, but only when they appeared within the magic circle of psychology; next moment, when the spotlight cast its beam elsewhere, there was nothing to be seen" (p. 357).

Both when I said that in the situations described before, psychotherapy was in the grip of the ego and with my references to Freud and Jung, my discussion remained on the personal level of *people's psychology*. But psychotherapy can also be in the grip of the ego in an objective sense, that is, in its own logical form. This is the case when it is conceived as a healing and helping profession. No doubt, in an empirical, practical sense the *external* purpose of psychotherapy is to help and possibly cure patients. But within itself, in its own logical constitution, it does not have to have an external purpose at all, although it *can*, no doubt, well be subsumed under this purpose and defined as being in itself a healing profession. The second possibility means that it is objectively, structurally, in the grip of the ego. It then follows the motto: "instead of psychology, use of psychological means..." (*Letters 1*, p.535, to Thompson, 23 September 1949). The point we need to make here again, as explained in the "Preamble" and Chapters II and III above, is that it is not the therapists who have to bring healing but solely the soul. The psychological mistake of the egoic misconstrual of psychotherapy is that ego desires and intentions are smuggled into the logic of psychotherapy itself. It becomes a technology. Psychotherapy is not released from our human wishes and not released into *itself*, into its own logic, into *psychology* or psychology-making.

So far I explained the belief in the healing power of psychotherapy from ego wishes, be it the personal psychic needs of individual therapists to cure people and remove their suffering or be it the objective ego concern about healing instilled, or inflated, into the logical structure of psychotherapy as such. But we also need to understand what this belief and hope means in itself, not only what drives it.

The fantasy of *healing as such* expresses a disregard of, and disrespect for, the reality of *the other* and the *otherness* of the other. It proceeds from the tacit notion that the domain of the therapeutic ego as a matter of course would extend over the patient's illness and the patient himself. The "other" is pocketed, a priori prepossessed. Logically (of course not empirically), the fantasy of healing has always already construed the disorders as lying within its sphere of influence, as in principle *manageable*. This is what makes this kind of therapy intrinsically technological. It is part of the science fantasy of nature. Scientific consciousness has on principle taken the logical position of the creator god, *under* whose rule everything natural or empirical exists. Explicitly nature is of course still largely unknown and in many ways still unpredictable for the scientific mind. But logically and implicitly it is already fully known, and this is the condition of the possibility a priori for the human scientist's attempt to empirically and practically step by step *catch up with* the full knowledge of the world that according to its logic always already exists. The book of nature has already been written and is concluded. The human reader, however, is still somewhere in the middle of the book and has not reached the end yet. In a similar way psychotherapy, conceived as healing profession, has *logically* overreached whatever is to be cured, even if practically it still needs to bring about the factual cure.

The false attitudes of consciousness, the complexes, the neurotic structures, and the very *nature* of patients are not seen as hard facts, real realities, rock-like, very unlikely to change. Implicitly they are viewed "idealistically" as if they were free-floating fantasies, images, conceptions, opinions that merely through analysis, seeing-through, or through argumentation and re-imagining as well as through empathy could be corrected or replaced by better ones. And the soul of other persons is not viewed as *fundamentally* (not only empirically) out of reach.

The other in its otherness needs to be released into itself. It needs to be let free, honored in its own untouchable dignity.[95] What was discussed above in Chapter IV.4 about healing through

---

95 This is the virtue of Heinrich Fierz's and Adolf Guggenbühl-Craig's insistence on the idea that therapy at best merely "*constellates*" healing. Despite the mystifying and substantiating introduction of a "healer archetype" as what is allegedly being constellated, this view preserves the untouchable dignity of the other. If we drop the "healer archetype" and stick to the simple notion of constellating per se, it describes well all that psychotherapy can do: *deo concedente*. As Jung said: "I do nothing; there is nothing I can do except wait, with a certain trust in God, until, out of a conflict borne with patience and fortitude, there emerges that particular, for me unforeseeable, solution that is destined for that particular person" (*CW* 12 § 37, transl. modif.). And yet, he says, he is not "passive or inactive", he "help[s] the patient to understand all the things that the unconscious produces during the conflict".

one's allowing oneself to be the way one really is and about the 'perfect tense' of one's individual true nature applies *mutatis mutandis* to the present topic. To begin with, the unlikeliness of a psychological cure, of people's possibility to change needs to be seen. We must not reckon without our host. People and their attitudes or complexes are for the most part not dough ready to be kneaded, neither by the therapist nor even by the patients themselves. The patients are already baked, finished, shaped and set in their shape by their nature and their history.

A patient's neurosis may have been thoroughly analyzed, its structure and the very neuroticness and destructiveness of the neurosis may have been clearly laid bare, and all this may even have been clearly understood by the patient in his consciousness, but nevertheless only all too often to no avail. The understanding remains a purely intellectual one on the upper level, the level of ego-consciousness, but is not *echoed* in and taken over by *the other* in the patient and does not *reverberate* from that place where the *reality* of the neurosis is anchored. As ego-personality the patient may have become able to thoroughly see through, comprehend and truly distance himself from the structure of his neurosis and the underlying neurotic spiteful insistence. But the neurosis does not disappear if it is not the patient as "whole man" (*homo totus*) who has reached this comprehension.

The psychotherapist may be able to successfully help the patient to achieve such an intellectual understanding. But with respect to a *real* understanding that in fact makes a difference he (just as much as his patient) is helpless. It is not in their power to bring it about, to make the penny drop. It is something only the objective soul can do. Whether it happens or not is a matter of fate, not of therapy.

This is why we need as psychologists a great modesty, humility. Logically, psychotherapy should ultimately be comprehended as a *helpless* profession, by which I do not mean that it is useless and cannot lead to cures. What I mean is that the idea of healing and helping should be struck from its self-definition, because as therapists we only do our job as a kind of craft,[96] but

---

96 Many psychic problems that are relatively close to consciousness can be consciously resolved. Here the therapist is only needed as a craftsman, and the issue of "healing" does not arise in the first place. Some patients only need a portion of common sense, as Jung already said. Soul is not involved.

the healing is not our business. Ethically, we have to start out from the acknowledgment that every patient is possibly a "hopeless case". Only then do we respect him as a reality and have we ourselves fully given up our claim to being healers, and only on this basis can a professional therapy begin that leaves it to the soul if any healing will happen. Indirectness. The mystery of healing must be left intact.

What, as I said above using a Hegel quote[97], needs to be brought to the patient, also needs to become psychotherapy's own attitude, especially in view of the experience that patients are already "baked", their disorders "hard facts": Psychotherapy needs to be conducted with a mindset of necessity. It needs to say to itself: It is so, nothing can be done about it; I must put up with it. By standing on this standpoint and saying: that's the way it is, it must have put aside every particularity, have renounced and abstracted from all special purposes, interests. There is no consolation for man (therapist and patient alike) available but also not needed. Consolation is needed only in so far as we demand compensation for the experienced loss[98] or for the lot we have to carry; we, as *psychologists*, must have given up the inner root of what has been lost. And what we have given up, we must have completely given up.

Such an attitude might be a good precondition for healing happening of its own accord, for allowing the soul take over.

---

97 See footnote 83.
98 The loss of what hope and wishful thinking promised to us.

Other Titles in English by Wolfgang Giegerich

The Soul's Logical Life: Towards a Rigorous Notion of Psychology, Frankfurt am Main, et al. (Peter Lang) 1998, 5th edition revised and extended by an index, 2020.

(with David L. Miller, Greg Mogenson) *Dialectics and Analytical Psychology: The El Capitan Canyon Seminar*, New Orleans (Spring Journal Books) 2005.

The Neurosis of Psychology. Primary Papers towards a Critical Psychologie. CEP 1 (2006.)

Technology and the Soul. From the Nuclear Bomb to the World Wide Web. CEP 2 (2007).

Soul-Violence. CEP 3 (2008).

The Soul Always Thinks. CEP 4 (2010).

What Is Soul? New Orleans, LA (Spring Journal Books) 2012.

The Flight Into The Unconscious. An Analysis of C.G. Jung's Psychology Project CEP 5 (2013).

Neurosis. The Logic of a Metaphysical Illness, New Orleans, LA (Spring Journal Books) 2013.

"Dreaming the Myth Onwards": C.G. Jung on Christianity and on Hegel. Part 2 of The Flight Into the Unconscious CEP 6 (2013).

Pitfalls in Comparing Buddhist and Western Psychology: A contribution to psychology's self-clarification, ISPDI Monograph Series, vol. 2, CreateSpace Independent Publishing Platform, 2018.

The Historical Emergence of the I. Essays about one Chapter of the History of the Soul, London, Ontario (Dusk Owl Books) 2020.

Made in the USA
Las Vegas, NV
11 April 2022

47222061R00079